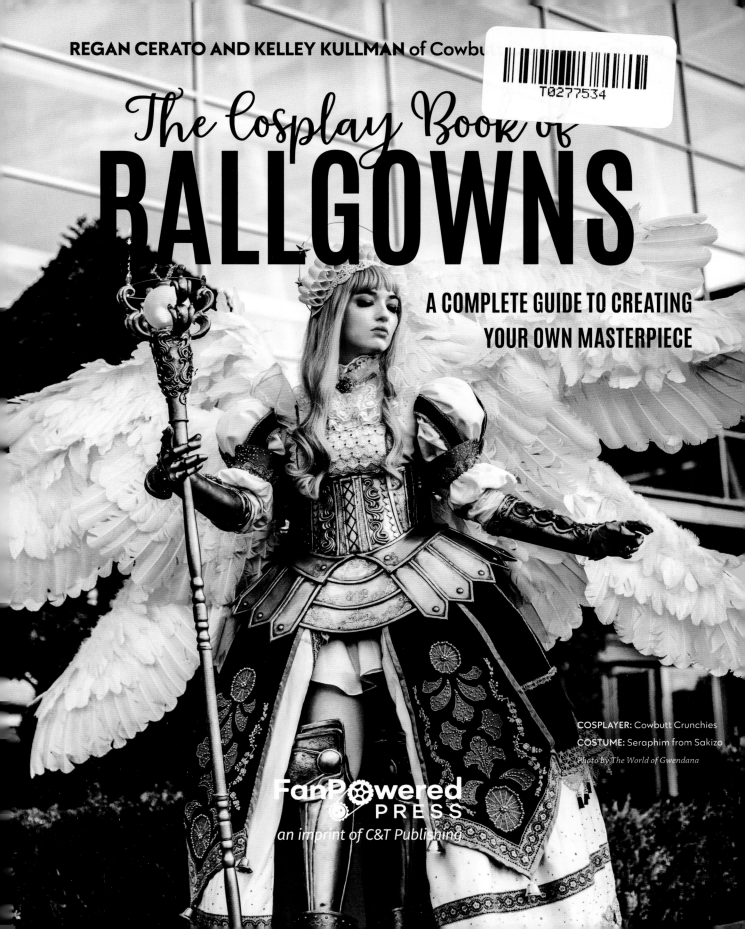

REGAN CERATO AND KELLEY KULLMAN of Cowbu[tt]

The Cosplay Book of
BALLGOWNS

A COMPLETE GUIDE TO CREATING
YOUR OWN MASTERPIECE

COSPLAYER: Cowbutt Crunchies
COSTUME: Seraphim from Sakizo
Photo by The World of Gwendana

FanPowered
PRESS
an imprint of C&T Publishing

Text and artwork copyright © 2022 by Regan Cerato and Kelley Kullman

Artwork copyright © 2022 by C&T Publishing, Inc.

Publisher: Amy Barrett-Daffin

Creative Director: Gailen Runge

Senior Editor: Roxane Cerda

Editors: Beth Baumgartel and Liz Aneloski

Technical Editor: Helen Frost

Cover/Book Designer: April Mostek

Production Coordinator: Tim Manibusan

Illustrator: Linda Johnson

Photography Assistant: Gabriel Martinez

Cover photography by Amie Photos_

Instructional photography by Regan Cerato and Kelley Kullman

Styled photography as noted

Floral Patterns provided by Ozz Design/Shutterstock.com

Published by FanPowered Press, an imprint of C&T Publishing, Inc., P.O. Box 1456, Lafayette, CA 94549

Library of Congress Cataloging-in-Publication Data

Names: Cerato, Regan, 1983- author. | Kullman, Kelley, 1985- author.

Title: The cosplay book of ballgowns : a complete guide to creating your own masterpiece / Regan Cerato and Kelley Kullman of Cowbutt Crunchies Cosplay.

Description: Lafayette, CA : FanPowered Press, an imprint of C&T Publishing, [2022] | Summary: "Learn how to create your own fairytale masterpieces from scratch with different techniques on silhouette, planning, patterning, construction and more. From elegant princesses to dramatic sorcerers, ballgowns are a crucial part of any cosplayer's wardrobe"-- Provided by publisher.

Identifiers: LCCN 2022021110 | ISBN 9781644031933 (trade paperback) | ISBN 9781644031940 (ebook)

Subjects: LCSH: Costume design. | Cosplay--Equipment and supplies. | Dresses. | Dressmaking.

Classification: LCC TT633 .C46 2022 | DDC 746.9/2--dc23/eng/20220705

LC record available at https://lccn.loc.gov/2022021110

Printed in the USA

10 9 8 7 6 5 4 3

COSPLAYER: Cowbutt Crunchies
COSTUME: Loki from *Thor* (original design)
Photo by Sam Saturn

Dedication

Dedicated to our cats, our families, and also to our cosplay family! You're the best!

ACKNOWLEDGMENTS

A huge thank-you to the amazing photographers we've met throughout the years—Kyle, Sarah, Sam, Amie, Alex, Charles, Lenore, David, and Nate. And, of course, to the fantastic cosplayers who contributed their works and words to this book: You're all an inspiration!

Our cosplay family

Photo by Mineralblu

CONTENTS

COSPLAYER: Cowbutt Crunchies
COSTUME: Seraphim from Sakizo
Photo by Alexandra Lee Studios

For many, cosplay is about extravagance and creating larger-than-life outfits. And there's nothing more extravagant than the indomitable ballgown! Ballgowns can be found in all corners of pop culture and historical reenactment, from superpowered princesses to ladies in waiting. Beloved by master cosplayers and novices alike, ballgowns are a favorite due to their versatility and variety.

INTRODUCTION

COSPLAYER: Ilabelle Cosplay

COSTUME: Belle from *Beauty and the Beast*

Photo by Mama Kat Photography

Create the Cosplay Ballgown of Your Dreams!

Don't be intimidated by their size! These monster gowns can be broken down into easy-to-understand components, which, once assembled, come together to create a head-to-toe garment that looks fantastic on cosplayers of all shapes and sizes. At its core, a ballgown is composed of three main pieces: the undergarments, the bodice, and the skirt. However, your choices don't end there; selecting the style of these main pieces heavily influences both the level of sewing difficulty, as well as the final gown shape!

As long time cosplayers who adore these fabulous dresses, we've created our fair share of ballgowns over the years, from original designs to re-creations to historical silhouettes. In this book we hope to provide a one-stop resource to help guide newcomers and experienced cosplayers alike toward creating the gowns of their dreams!

COSPLAYER: Cowbutt Crunchies

COSTUMES: Princess Bubblegum and Marceline from *Adventure Time* (original designs)

Photo by Charles Lan Photography

BALLGOWN BASICS

COSPLAYER: Cowbutt Crunchies

COSTUMES: Necromancer and Apprentice from Sakizo

Photo by Sam Saturn

Ballgown Anatomy

What exactly is a ballgown? While most people have a good idea of what a "classic" ballgown is, understanding the pieces and construction methods helps explain why there is such a huge variety of dresses in different styles, periods, and levels of formality.

Not all gowns are created equal! From classic Disney styles to modern, sleek dresses to historically influenced garments, changes in the bodice, undergarments, skirts, and embellishments can create drastic changes in the overall look and feel of your cosplay! Translating a two-dimensional or fictional character's design requires understanding not just the basic anatomy of a ballgown, but things like silhouette and proportion.

Understanding the basic parts of a ballgown is an important start in the journey of ballgown creation.

COSPLAYER: Cowbutt Crunchies

COSTUME: Helgasercle
from *Tree of Savior*

Photo by Sam Saturn

UNDERGARMENTS

Any layer of your garment that isn't the finished dress layer is an undergarment. The goal of undergarments is to create structure under your finished dress to achieve certain shapes and sizes, or to modify your body in certain ways.

CORSET Corsets are boned garments for the upper part of the body, designed to shape the waist and bust area. While the word *corset* as a technical term refers to a relatively modern garment and build, in cosplay, the word often refers to anything from sixteenth-century bodices to eighteenth-century stays (fully boned undergarments) to modern, cupped fashion corsets designed to be worn on the outside. Whether worn as underwear or incorporated into a fantastical bodice, they are useful, and beautiful, in a huge variety of designs.

HOOP SKIRT/BUSTLE Skirts that are worn as one of the innermost layers of a ballgown are referred to as *hoop skirts*. They are highly structured garments which use boning and sewn channels to create a variety of shapes and sizes, which in turn support heavy skirts. Traditional hoop skirts go under the entire skirt, while bustles usually only add support to the back of a skirt. Like corsets, the shape and build of hoop skirts has changed through history, but cosplay has adopted them as a must-have for mighty silhouettes.

PETTICOAT/CRINOLINE Underskirts, often worn over hoop skirts but sometimes by themselves, are designed to provide body and volume under a finished skirt. They also come in a variety of shapes, to match the variety of skirt shapes, and are often made of organza or net fabric.

MODERN UNDERGARMENTS   Items like bras, body shapers, binders, padded shorts—while these are less traditional ballgown garments—there's no rule that says they don't work! For example, a good bra and shapewear can swap out for a corset. Modern undergarments can be an excellent option if you're pressed for time or materials—and can also help if you have a limited budget.

BODICE AND SKIRT

A bodice is the shirt or top portion of a dress. This can be attached to the skirt, or not. In cosplay, a bodice can be a simple fitted bustier, a full corset decorated to be outerwear, a heavily structured shirt with sleeves and a collar, or anything between. A bodice can include sleeves, armor attachments, and faux openings, and it is often where some of the best detailing happens!

The skirt is the bottom portion of the dress. This can be attached to the top portion to create a "true" dress, or it can be made as a stand-alone skirt with a separate top, which is often much more practical for cosplay ballgowns. In this book when we discuss skirts, this can include a single skirt, layered skirts, a skirt with a faux layering, or skirts with trains, bustles, and swags. While the possibilities are endless, the construction basics remain the same.

Getting Started

There are many important but fundamental aspects of a gown that impact how it looks and feels. They include the following:

- Skirt shape (including the shape of hoops and petticoats)
- Overall skirt volume and skirt length
- Corset shape and bodice shape
- Neckline style
- Sleeve style and length
- Waist length (where the waistline hits)
- Whether the gown is purely fantastical or whether it references a specific historical period
- Fabric type, weight, and color choices
- Embellishment types and placement

And of course, since this is cosplay, there are always special, extra, character-specific items to incorporate to really bring the ballgown to life.

While we discuss these details in more depth in each relevant chapter, it's important to think about the overall design from the beginning. As you read through this book, feel free to mix, match, and be creative with different elements according to your source materials and design preferences!

COSPLAYER: Cowbutt Crunchies
COSTUME: Machine Queen
(original design)

Photo by Para Para Productions

Sweetheart, drop waist boned bodice

Bell skirt over round hoop

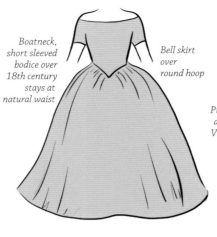

Boatneck, short sleeved bodice over 18th century stays at natural waist

Bell skirt over round hoop

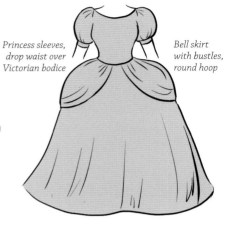

Princess sleeves, drop waist over Victorian bodice

Bell skirt with bustles, round hoop

Examples of how mixing different elements can truly create a custom, one-of-a-kind cosplay ballgown.

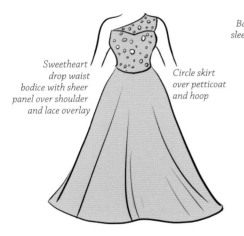

Sweetheart drop waist bodice with sheer panel over shoulder and lace overlay

Circle skirt over petticoat and hoop

Bodice with puffed sleeves over modern undergarments

High empire-waist circle skirt

Corseted bodice with support for wings

Bell-shape short skirt over petticoat

Long bell-sleeved bodice over modern cupped corset with scoop neck

Half-circle skirt over petticoat

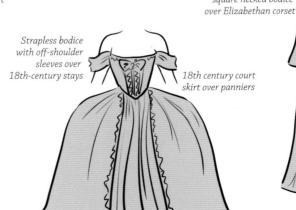

Strapless bodice with off-shoulder sleeves over 18th-century stays

18th century court skirt over panniers

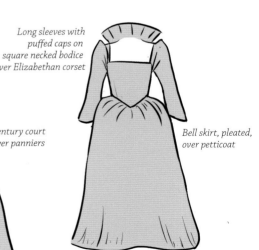

Long sleeves with puffed caps on square necked bodice over Elizabethan corset

Bell skirt, pleated, over petticoat

TIPS AND TECHNIQUES

Consider these tips and tricks before getting started.

* Know your skill level. We love seeing ambitious cosplayers! Ballgowns come in all levels of difficulty, but some are more difficult than others. If you are a new or novice cosplayer, consider first tackling a simpler bodice or a simpler skirt shape before upgrading to a more difficult corset or historical-era garment. Practicing the basics gives you the confidence and experience that will help make future projects a breeze!

* Know your time limitations. Ballgowns are complex. You will likely need several weeks to several months to complete your cosplay, depending on your speed, your skills, and the complexity of your project. Schedule enough time before a deadline so that you are not forced to rush, especially if you are newer to ballgown construction.

* Remember that the end goal is to create a gown that you will wear—sometimes for hours, in busy, crowded convention spaces. Never hesitate to make design changes to make yourself more comfortable, whether that's scaling down the size of a truly huge design, adjusting a revealing neckline, swapping shoes, or forgoing extreme waist cinching. Cosplay should always be fun, and your comfort is more important than accuracy.

* While many cosplayers joke that planning the cosplay is when all the fun happens, we firmly believe that a thorough plan of attack is what keeps you having fun through the whole process! Nothing is worse than getting partway through making a costume and running out of fabric or realizing your costume pieces don't work as a coherent whole, or that you need to undo completed work to properly include a decorative element. As part of building your cosplay plan, we encourage you to read through this book for an understanding of the entire process before starting any actual sewing.

COSPLAYER: Cowbutt Crunchies
COSTUME: The Forest Spirit from *Princess Mononoke* (original design)
Photo by Amie Photos

Cosplay Creative: Pearly Bae Cosplay

Instagram: @PearlyBaeCosplay

I am a lover of books, DnD, and costumes! I work professionally in the theatre/film/TV industry as a costumer during the day, all while making cosplays for myself in my spare time.

With over ten years of experience, my relationship with costumes has always stemmed from a love of how the visual impact of a beautiful dress can contribute to bringing a story to life. Being able to bring out the heart of a character in the clothes they wear is something I think is important and something I strive for in both the making and the wearing of a beautiful gown.

One of the most important things in creating any costume is the thought and research that goes into the making of it. Reference the original source material, but don't let it limit you either! Experiment and manipulate different kinds of materials and techniques to help bring your vision to life! Cosplay is all about innovation and creativity, breaking walls and manifesting those incredible designs into the real world.

TIPS

- Be mindful of gilding the lily; one of the pitfalls in dress creation is getting carried away with extravagance and losing sight of the character within the frills. Remember, *you* must be able to wear the dress, and not the other way around.

- Dressmaking can be a little daunting if you're a beginner, so don't be afraid to make mistakes, and ask for help if you need it.

- Take your time, be kind to yourself, and enjoy the entirety of the process from the beginning to the end! Let the journey bring you joy, and you will be delighted in the destination you reach.

COSPLAYER: Pearly Bae Cosplay

COSTUME: The Voidfish from *The Adventure Zone* (original design)

Photo by Sam Saturn

PLAN YOUR PROJECT

COSPLAYER: Cowbutt Crunchies

COSTUME: Princess Bubblegum
from *Adventure Time*
(original design)

Photo by The World of Gwendana

Creating a Project / Design Plan

So, your favorite character wears a ballgown. Great! Now what? While running out to buy fabric and trim is tempting, ballgowns are complex projects, and creating a general costume plan first sets you up for success throughout the whole project! This includes looking at your sources, making fabric decisions, deciding on general costume proportions, selecting patterns as needed, and having a general understanding of how you'll approach your pieces and in which order. For each individual element of a ballgown, we've included more specific planning information, patterning advice, and construction tips in the relevant chapter.

INTERPRETING SOURCES

A vitally important part of cosplay is understanding the type of ballgown your character wears. Gather as many references (source materials) as possible that show the gown from the front, side, and back, and in motion. Take a close look at all your references and ask yourself questions about the shape of the ballgown, as well as important details. Questions such as these:

Drawing by
Regan Cerato

* Does the character live in a certain era or real-life location? Is the gown also based on historical garments?

* How voluminous should the gown be? Will you want to match the source exactly, or make alterations for practicality's sake?

* What is the skirt silhouette? Does the skirt flow or is it more structured? Are there any references showing multiple angles—can you see petticoats or other undergarments? Will you need to add structure even if it's not in the source material?

* How structured is the bodice? Does it fit the character's natural form? Will you want to include body-shaping aspects, such as waist reduction, bust padding, and the like?

* Are there sleeves? A cape? Do you need to pattern (plan) your bodice to include attachment points or armhole openings? How will this affect construction of the rest of the bodice?

* How heavy will the embellishments be? Will they be sewn to the gown itself, or do they need more support due to weight, size, material? Should you forgo a separate bodice and fashion a corset to better support those elements?

* Are there any especially fantastic aspects to the dress? Is it based more on "real" garments or are there aspects that only work in illustration? How interpretive can you go—if the character's gown is made of fire, for example, is there a fabric you can use that looks similar?

* Does the design have clear construction clues? Are there obvious seams that should be duplicated? Are there obvious closures, and are they drawn in a way that they truly should be functional closures?

COSPLAYER: Sky Gets Fancy

COSTUME: The Spaceship Earth globe at Disney's Epcot (original design)

ORIGINAL DESIGNS

One of our favorite ways to get creative is to create original ballgown designs! These cosplays are re-creations of characters we love, but with a twist: We design them from scratch! Original designs allow you to really flex your creativity and pay homage to characters whose in-show costumes you may not want to recreate. In the past we've created ballgown versions of Princess Bubblegum from *Adventure Time*, Ms. Frizzle from *The Magic School Bus*, and Deku Princess from *The Legend of Zelda*—however, the possibilities are endless!

Your steps for constructing an original design follow the same path as those for any other ballgown. Consult Interpreting Sources (page 17) to decide what shape, look, and feel you want for your original gown. Consider your character's personality and style while you answer these questions: Is the character light and sweet, or do they have a darker edge? Would they go for over-the-top sparkle and pouf, or are they about clean lines and subtle details? Are there iconic parts of the character's normal design you can incorporate as accessories, or reinterpret in a new way? Your love and understanding of the character should have the largest effect on your ballgown's shape and feel.

Original designs have been exploding in popularity in the cosplay community. If you're intrigued but not up for the task of designing your own, numerous artists create ready-to-cosplay designs for all sorts of properties!

As you figure out the design details which are most important, browse through this book for details on shapes, construction methods, and what to look out for. Have a general idea of what undergarments you plan to make, if there are any character- or design-specific pitfalls to look for, what materials you need, key measurements to take, and how you intend to pattern and plan your garment.

COSPLAYER:
Cowbutt Crunchies

COSTUME: Marceline
from *Adventure Time*
(original design)

Photo by Sorairo Days

Tools, Notions and Supplies, Fabrics

SEWING TOOLS

Creating a ballgown involves many of the same sewing tools you use for creating any other cosplay. Common tools we recommend every sewist, crafter, and cosplayer have at hand are the following:

Basic Sewing Tools

Scissors—at least one pair for fabric only, and one pair for other materials

Needles—machine and hand sewing

Pins, Wonder Clips, or other pin-alternative clips

Iron and ironing board

Erasable or disappearing-ink fabric pens or dressmaker's chalk, regular pens/markers

Extra-large format paper or poster board for pattern drafting

Aerosol basting spray

Rulers, including a large yard or meter stick for skirt patterning, a see-through dressmaking ruler, and a flexible measuring tape

Calculator for figuring out proportions, pattern adjustments, and so on.

It is also helpful to keep a selection of common notions on hand. They include hook and eye closures, eyelets, grommets, grosgrain ribbon or twill tape, interfacing, horsehair braid, cotton webbing or strapping, snaps, and an assortment of zippers. To attach grommets, snaps, or eyelets, you'll need an awl and the appropriate setting tools.

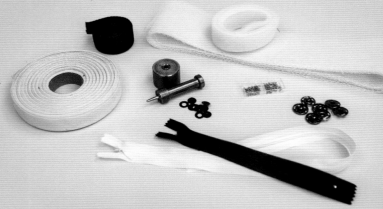

CORSETRY AND HOOP SKIRT SUPPLIES

While many of the materials needed for creating a gorgeous gown are familiar to most cosplayers, some of the materials for the special undergarments might not be. Corsets and hoop skirts, due to their heavily-structured nature, require specialty materials. Corset lacing and two-part grommets are discussed in greater detail in the Undergarments chapter (page 45). Boning, however, is almost always used in corsets, so it is good to become familiar with the various options and related supplies.

Boning is sold in rigid strips of either special plastic or metal (also called *hoopsteel*) and is designed to provide structural support in garments. It is used in corsets, hoop skirts, and bodices, as needed for extra support.

Boning casing tape has a channel for the actual boning and is a quick way to add boning into a garment.

Boning tips are special horseshoe-shaped pieces of metal you can buy from the same supplier as the boning, in the same standard sizes as the boning.

Busks are designed to go into the center front of a corset and can be either a single rigid piece (common in pre-1800s historical styles) or two pieces, with metal hooks and pins, and are designed to allow the corset to open and close in the front as well as the back.

Lacing tape has pre-installed grommets and is designed for a laced garment opening.

Metal boning requires *heavy cutting tools*, such as tin snips or bolt cutters, to trim the boning to the correct length. When you apply boning tips, standard hardware store *pliers* are sufficient. Plastic boning can often be cut with sturdy scissors.

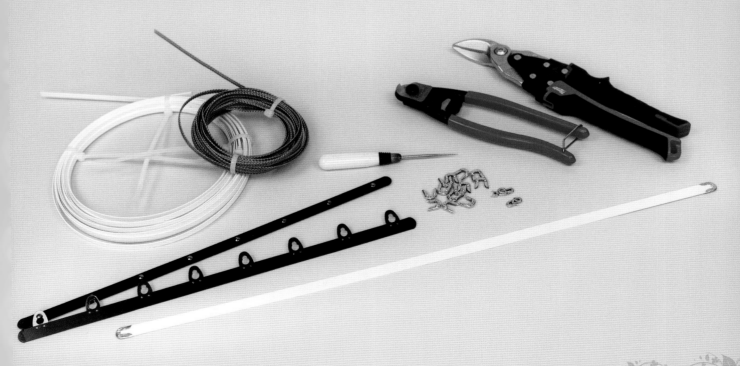

Hoopsteel

Plastic

Spiral steel

Flat steel (corsetry width)

Types of Boning

Corsetry boning is heavy duty and strong enough to shape your body, and comes in three general varieties. Be careful when selecting boning—there are types of boning often sold at sewing supply stores called either "featherlight" or "rigilene." These types can be used to add structure to simple everyday garments like shirts, but they *should not* be used for corsetry because they are too flimsy. When in doubt, buy from a reputable corset supply vendor so you get the right product.

GERMAN PLASTIC/SYNTHETIC WHALEBONE   A specialty plastic boning designed specifically for corsets and only available from corsetry retailers. It is stronger and less likely to deform in heat. It is a super lightweight product that is easy to cut and finish. Since it's plastic, it's washable. We like to use this in corsets that aren't designed for major waist reduction, or as boning in bodices for a bit of extra structure, or in corset styles that require a larger number of bones.

SPIRAL STEEL   A type of boning made from tightly coiled wire that bends in multiple directions, making it perfect for the complex curves of more modern corset shapes. This is an excellent material to use for long-lasting, durable corsets. It comes in a variety of widths—we recommend ¼" (6mm), which is widely available at specialty vendors and can be purchased as pre-cut and pre-tipped or uncut on a long roll.

FLAT/SPRING STEEL   A flat type of steel that only bends in one direction. As a result, it's excellent for areas where you need a curve in one direction but rigid strength in another, such as at the back opening of a corset. Spring steel also comes in the same standard widths that spiral does and uses the same style of tips to finish. This material, when sold in larger widths, is also called *hoopsteel* or *hoop boning*, and is used in hoop skirts to provide structure. The only difference is the width of the material: ¼" for corsetry, and widths around ½" for hoop skirts.

Tip

We recommend German plastic, synthetic whalebone, or larger-sized zip ties for boning a bodice (page 47). Plastic materials are easier to work with than steel, and bodices often don't need the long-lasting durability of steel bones.

Note

There is also a product called hoop wire *or* tutu wire *that is designed for the large, very flat-style tutu skirts ballet dancers wear and is not generally sturdy enough for full-size ballgown hoop skirts. It is thinner than standard hoop steel—only ⅜" wide instead of ½" wide—so check the measurements of the hooping material before you buy it!*

Handling Boning

Most boning, unless you buy it pre-cut to the exact length you need, must be cut to fit your corset, which means you also need to finish the cut edges. Each type of boning is finished differently.

German plastic boning is the easiest to finish. Because it's plastic, use a sharp pair of scissors to trim off the sharp corners, and then a bit of sandpaper or a nail file to make the edges smoother.

Steel boning is a little more complex to finish. Cutting requires heavier tools designed to cut metal—we use a pair of tin snips from the hardware store, but you can also use a rotary tool if you have one. This usually means the boning has a blunt edge where it's been cut. This is where *boning tips* come into play. They are designed to slide over the sharp metal edges of both spring and spiral steel. Once on, use a pair of pliers to crimp the tip firmly onto the bone, so it doesn't slip off while the bone is inserted into the corset. The boning tips completely smooth out the ends of the bone.

Tip

Having finished ends is extremely important, since each bone is under pressure in the corset and raw sharp edges will eventually rub and rip through the fabric of your corset, damaging the garment and possibly scratching you.

Note: About Zip Ties

Many cosplayers use heavy-duty zip ties, available from hardware stores, as a budget replacement for real corset boning. While this can certainly work, there are some downsides: Zip ties don't have the same heat resistance as real boning and can deform over time. They are also thicker and wider than corset materials. This means you might not be able to use boning tape, which comes in standard sizes. Ultimately, we recommend investing in specialty materials when making a corset that is truly designed to be worn as underwear for many different costumes. Save the zip ties for additional boning in bodices or for corsets which are designed to be the bodice and are costume specific.

FABRICS

A beautiful gown deserves to be made of beautiful fabrics! Avoid thin, matte cottons or ultra-shiny satins, which appear flat and/or inexpensive-looking. Instead, formal fabrics with a moderate to high sheen are a favorite choice among cosplayers. High-quality silk fabrics may come with a hefty price tag, but not all gown fabric needs to be expensive! When budgeting, look in discount or remnant fabric stores, or search for high-quality polyester imitations.

If you order fabrics online, try to purchase a sample first to guarantee that the color and weight match your project vision. See Resources and Supplies (page 127) for some of our favorite fabric suppliers.

Tip

Silk Satin? Imitation Dupioni? Polyester Silk?

When deciding on fabrics, there are two major factors to consider: fabric weave and fiber content. Many of the suggested fabrics are listed by weave, and come in a variety of fibers—velvet, for example, can be made from silk, cotton, wool, or polyester, all with their own price point. Generally, natural fibers—fibers that come from plants or animals—are considered more luxurious than synthetic fibers like polyester and nylon. Natural fibers tend to breathe better and feel nicer, are usually easier to launder, and last a long time without showing wear and tear.

That isn't to say you absolutely must rush out and purchase 100% silk for every aspect of your costume! Cosplayers often mix and match fibers and use different fabrics due to their different qualities: For example, a haunted or ghostly character, with large areas of distressing and ragged edges, would be better served by polyester, which can be heat-sealed during distressing. On the other hand, there are definitely cases when using natural fibers is beneficial—real cotton, for example, is excellent for making hoop skirts and lining corsets, because it's a breathable fabric that doesn't trap heat.

Regardless of whether you want to use synthetic or natural fabrics, your fabric should be purchased with intention. Sometimes it's hard to tell what fibers were used to make a fabric and the amount of "imitation silk"—aka polyester dupioni or shantung, which are weaves strongly associated with silk—being sold has muddied the water. Any fabric you purchase should have both the fiber content and the weave listed. If it doesn't, it's likely to be polyester, or at least a blend. One way to tell what fibers make up a fabric is to use a lighter to carefully burn a small scrap of the fabric—if it catches and turns into ashes, it's most likely a natural fiber. If it shrinks up and gets a solid edge where it's burned, it's most likely a synthetic. Blends produce both ash and a sealed edge.

Types of Fabric

Consider how you want your ball-gown to flow and feel. The following fabrics vary in weight, stiffness, drape, texture, and shine, which greatly affects the look, drape, and feel of your finished cosplay.

CHIFFON   While not heavy enough for bodices or structural layers, sheer, semi-transparent chiffon can be gathered or layered over more opaque fabrics to create a soft, ethereal effect. It's excellent for full skirts with lots of drape that are meant to feel light and airy.

COSPLAYER:
Cowbutt Crunchies

Costume: Fluttershy
from *My Little Pony*
(original design)

*Photo by Nate Buchman
Photography*

CHARMEUSE Lightweight but opaque, charmeuse is ultra-silky with a high sheen. A slippery fabric, it shines on draped designs.

COTTON AND LINEN While less suitable for extravagant ballgowns, a subtly textured cotton or linen weave is a great choice for a less formal gown or a historical costume. Look for high-quality cottons, sateens, or reenactment-inspired fabrics.

Tip

We suggest using a light or medium-weight cotton fabric as lining for corsets and bodices as it is both comfortable and breathable. A sturdy, medium weight cotton is also an excellent choice for constructing hoop skirts or waistbands.

COUTIL, TWILL, AND DUCK CLOTH These fabrics are perfect for the interlining layer of a corset to help maintain the shape of the corset over time and help it to resist warping. Coutil is a tightly woven, dense fabric with little to no stretch designed especially for corset making. If coutil is unavailable, a tightly woven non-stretch twill or a heavy duck cloth are suitable substitutes.

DUPIONI This fabric is a fantastic choice for structured, stiffer gowns or bodices. Dupioni is a very crisp fabric that falls in heavy folds. It has a noticeable slubbed texture and sometimes comes in interesting two-toned varieties.

ORGANZA Organza is thin, translucent fabric with a stiff hand. While it can be layered over opaque fabrics, it's a common choice for petticoats due to its light weight.

COSPLAYER: Cowbutt Crunchies
COSTUME: The Ugly Stepsisters from *Cinderella* (original design)
Photo by Elemental Photography

SATIN A smooth, glossy fabric with a soft hand, satin is manufactured in a wide variety of weights and shines. Cheap, lightweight polyester satin is only suitable for lining layers, while heavy duchess satin is more suitable for a luxurious skirt.

SHANTUNG Shantung combines dupioni's crispness with a smoother texture. This is another great choice for large skirts that require extra body.

TAFFETA Lightweight, but ultra-crisp, taffeta is smooth and glossy. This is an excellent choice for a bodice or skirt when a little extra shine is in order.

TULLE AND NETTING These fabrics are useful for quickly providing volume without any weight. They are commonly used to make petticoats and anywhere else pouf is needed. See Petticoats, page 56.

UPHOLSTERY FABRICS This is more of a category of fabrics than a single type of fabric. Upholstery fabrics are heavier fabrics, usually polyester, designed to be used in home decor and for covering furniture. They're often available in bold patterns with elaborate details, which can make them excellent for costumes that are historical or historically influenced. Many *Game of Thrones* cosplayers have tapped upholstery fabrics for their costumes. Because it is designed to be purchased in large amounts for furniture, it is often cheaper than equivalent jacquards or other fancy prints, so it makes a good budgetary option.

VELVET Heavy and luxurious, velvet's unique tufting gives this fabric a rich depth and softness. This is a fabric that requires extra care during cutting and handling to prevent crushing the pile.

Cosplay Creative: Raine Emery

Instagram: @raineemery

Making a ballgown doesn't have to be expensive for it to look good—materials can even come from items already found in the house. For my original design of Belle's ballgown from Disney's *Beauty and the Beast*, I used my mother's old curtains for the entirety of the skirt. And the best part? It didn't cost me a single penny! Try going to a local thrift store for fabric, jewelry, and additional accessories; you might find you can create a high-quality finished product at a fraction of the price.

The salmon-pink fabric I used for my Elizabethan-inspired Princess Peach ballgown was on discount at an upholstery fabric store, and the white diamond-patterned fabric was part of the two-yards-for-four-dollars section at Walmart. This proves that it is possible to create a magnificent gown on a budget. Sometimes I like to think of it as a game—what can I create with materials I already have, and what items can I find where someone least expects it (i.e., the thrift store, grocery store, etc.)?

COSPLAYER: Raine Emery
COSTUME: Princess Peach from *Mario Bros.* (original design)
Photo by Mapu Iosefa

Before You Sew

Once you have a general plan for moving forward with your design, including what undergarments you may need, the general silhouette, and how many elements will be included in the gown, you can begin adding details to your costume plan. While it's easy to jump in and start sewing, it is very important to think about how the pieces work together in terms of patterning, proportion, and construction, or you might end up with a lot of mismatched and ill-sized elements. The difference between a pretty dress and a stunning cosplay often comes down to how all the pieces of the costume *work together*, and whether your cosplay looks coherent.

Because much of a cosplay's final look is dependent on interior pieces that aren't even visible in the finished product, this book guides you from the inside out! However, because cosplayers are usually trying to re-create a specific look, we often find ourselves starting from that final look and planning our way backwards before we ever start sewing. It can be difficult, but it's important to look at a finished costume in your source material and try to figure out things like these: Do I need a hoop skirt or are petticoats alone enough? Should I make a corset? If so, should it include waist reduction for the silhouette I want? How much fabric do I need for a skirt that is sized and scaled to me? Do I want to add trim and how wide should that trim be?

These are *general* planning decisions you need to make early as part of your costume plan. These decisions form the foundation for a master plan as you work through each individual gown component listed in this book. This doesn't mean you can't make changes as you work, but having a master plan means you are always keeping the finished ballgown in mind.

MEASUREMENTS AND PROPORTIONS

Knowing your measurements and the desired proportions of the ballgown helps you purchase the correct amount of fabric, draft patterns, and buy accessories! You need your measurements both to purchase commercial patterns and to follow the instructions in this book for patterning your own petticoat or skirts. Think beyond the standard sewing measurements, like height, waist, shoulder width—and include costume-specific ones! How long do you want your skirt? How far out from your center should the fullest part of your dress be? How wide should a front panel on your bodice be? If the waist has been moved from your natural waist, how much higher or lower is it? Are you planning to make a corset, or wear high shoes?

It is very helpful to print a copy of the cosplay reference or design and mark important measurements directly on the printout. You can refer to it whenever you are making cutting and sewing decisions.

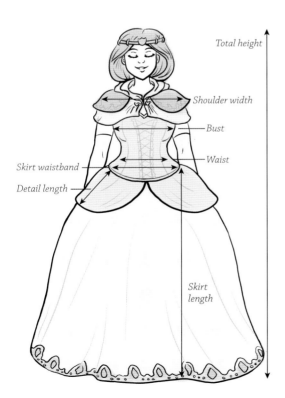

Accuracy is key when taking measurements! Measuring your hips, waist, and bust should be done with the measuring tape parallel to the floor all the way around, without dipping or tilting. Measuring across your shoulders or your waist-to-hip height should be done with neutral posture, without twisting or bending to get the tape measure in place. For this reason, it's often much easier to recruit a friend or family member to help you, although it can be done solo with the aid of a large mirror and plenty of patience. It's also important to measure your actual body—which means wearing undergarments during measuring, and not bulky clothing, which will throw your numbers off.

COSPLAYER: Bambi Lashes Design
COSTUME: Mipha from
The Legend of Zelda
(original design) ·
Photo by Felix Dandy

If you plan on purchasing under-garments which will change your measurements, such as an off-the-rack corset, body shaper, or padded undergarment, it's important to wear them during the measurement process, since they affect ballgown fit and fabric yardage. Treat these measurements as base measure-ments when choosing patterns or buying fabric.

If you plan to make your own corset or other undergarments, take your natural measurements to start. Most commercial corset patterns include instructions on how to pick a pattern size based on desired waist reduction and your unreduced waist measurement. A reduction of 1″–2″ is very common but consult your pattern!

Tip

Don't forget to account for shoes—the difference between ballet flats and 3″ heels is a big change to height-based measurements! It's fine to not have your final foot-wear but try to wear a pair that has similar heel height to your planned final shoes.

Finally, try to plan ahead for all accessories that might drastically change body or garment measure-ments, such as wing attachments, harnesses for armor or prosthetics, or other dramatic cosplay pieces.

Figuring Out Proportion

Cosplayers often have the additional challenge of re-creating beautiful designs from anime, comics, and illustrations where the characters aren't drawn as realistically proportioned figures. Anime characters especially tend to have impossibly long legs or thin waists, so translating their garments is difficult and there is often something that looks off. Proportion is an often-overlooked part of planning your costume but can really impact your finished garment. It is also difficult to go back and adjust proportion once you're deep into constructing your costume.

Your body measurements can be used to scale the original art (character references), and figure out how long or full to make your dress, where the waist should start, how poufed the sleeves should be, and so on. These aren't your finished measurements—rather, they're starting points to discuss sizing and patterning for your ballgown pieces.

Once you have your measurements, measure any important garment pieces of your planned cosplay, to determine the scale factor. Find the scale factor by dividing your height by the height of the figure. In this example, the cosplayer is just over 5′ 6″ (66.75″) and the figure in the art is 3.75″. So, the scale factor for the height is 17.8 (66.75″ divided by 3.75″).

In the illustration, the skirt width is 2.18″. Multiplying that by the scale factor of 17.8 yields approximately 38¾″ wide from side to side, so a total full circumference of about 76¾″. Now you should think about options to add that volume (see Undergarments, page 34).

Similarly, in the illustration, the skirt length is 1.58″. Scaled up to our cosplayer, the visual length of the finished cosplay skirt is approximately 28⅛″. Note this doesn't mean the actual length of the final skirt will be exactly 28⅛″ because the distance straight up and down from the waist to the floor is less than the diagonal distance, caused by structural undergar-ments that are much wider at the bottom. Rather, the 28⅛″ measurement is a final goal to work backwards from so that when all the pieces of the gown are together, the skirt should look 28⅛″ long to maintain the proportion.

You can use different body parts to scale different items on the costume; for example use your arm length to scale for bracers and your overall height for a cape! Your body can even be used to size small details like bows or bodice appliqués.

3¾″ Figure height

Scale factor = your height ÷ figure height

1.58″ Skirt height

66.75″ Your height

1.58″ × 17.8 = 28⅛ Skirt height

1. Measure your reference

2. Find the scale by dividing your height by the figure's height

3. Multiply the scale factor by the figure's measurements to find your matching measurement

2.18″ Skirt width

2.18″ × 17.8 = 38¾ Skirt width

The following ideas will help you visualize your cosplay and help proportion it for your body.

- Measure a string or ribbon and lay it in a circle matching your skirt circumference. Stand in the center and use a yardstick or have a friend use a measuring tape or other piece of ribbon to measure out to the "hem" you've marked. This requires a bit of imagination but is a good quick gut check, especially if you can tell immediately that you want your skirt much larger or smaller. This can help prevent wasted materials!

- Try on other costume or clothing pieces. For example, if your references and proportion math suggest 13″-long sleeves, try on a shirt with similar length and style sleeves for a quick visual comparison.

- For smaller pieces—such as sleeve flounces, accessories, and trim—draw them roughly on paper or scrap fabric and check them against your body in a mirror.

- For a very accurate visual, you can make a muslin (see Making a Muslin, page 33), although this is often more useful as a way to fine-tune measurements and sizing than when you are still in the early stages of planning.

When visualizing, consider: Does the proportion feel right? While the mathematical proportions are a great planning tool, they never need be set in stone! Cosplay is ultimately about being creative and designing a garment that you love, and love to wear, so if the mathematical answer doesn't feel or look right to you, feel free to make a creative choice. It's your cosplay, after all.

COSPLAYER: Cowbutt Crunchies

COSTUME: Ms. Frizzle from
The Magic School Bus (original design)

Photo by Reiukos Photography

PATTERNS

While we've included instructions in this book for drafting several of your own items—skirts, especially, can be very straightforward to draft yourself—there are lots of great commercial patterns out there for any gown design! While the most experienced sewists often have their own personal stash of self-drafted slopers, many times it can be easier to start with a pattern and alter it to your preferences.

When searching for patterns, be open-minded. Look past fabric choice and overall style to the garment elements themselves. Where are the seams and darts? How much structure is incorporated? What does the neckline look like? Is this pattern intended to be worn over a corset or hoop? Is the pattern referencing a certain historical period? Are there sleeves and can they be altered?

Knowing your body measurements, and having your project plan in mind, you can pick the correct pattern size, even if you know you might need to make alterations. The pattern also provides estimated yardage. See pattern suppliers in Resources and Supplies (page 127).

Making a Muslin

Whether you are using a commercial pattern or you've drafted one yourself, making a muslin draft is always a good idea. The muslin allows you to see and address fit, construction issues, and proportion decisions like length, waist placement, and fullness, all before using your expensive fabric. Be sure to make a separate test muslin for each fitted piece—the corset, bodice, and skirt. Hoop skirts and petticoats can be fine-tuned as you sew them, so they don't necessarily need a draft muslin. Muslins don't need to be completely finished (no zippers or button closings, only one sleeve, etc.). You can go back to them (or make new ones) as you make the bodice and skirt, and as you adjust your plan as your cosplay progresses.

Remember, when making fit adjustments, you need to wear the same body-shaping undergarments you wore when you took your measurements.

If you plan to wear a corset under the bodice and are making it yourself, you need to at least make the corset muslin first, to determine any fit or proportion changes. Make those changes until your finished muslin corset is in a wearable state before even starting the muslin of your bodice. A corset undergarment impacts the way the bodice fits. Also, if you plan on wearing a hoop skirt, you'll want to fit your skirt muslin over the hoop and petticoats. If you have time, it's best to complete your undergarments before starting your outer muslins.

The other benefit of a muslin is to allow pattern customizations on your body directly. For example—our Ms. Frizzle gown was originally drafted with a full bodice and shoulder seams. We drew a new strapless neckline, with a sheer top section, on the bodice muslin during fitting and then cut the various pieces apart, added seam allowances, and used the muslin pieces as pattern pieces. This allowed us to make the top portion of the bodice from a different fabric, but still have it fit perfectly!

Sometimes, the most important part of the outfit isn't the parts you see—it's what's on the inside that counts! In general, and in ballgowns specifically, cosplay undergarments have a huge impact on the finished product by changing the volume, silhouette, and structure of a gown. While undergarments can vary according to your design, the three biggest and most common items are corsets, hoop skirts, and petticoats. The combination creates a dress under your dress, and for especially large or elaborate gowns, they provide most of the structure.

UNDERGARMENTS

COSPLAYER: Cowbutt Crunchies
COSTUME: Seraphim from Sakizo
Photo by Sorairo Days

Corsets

Corsets make us recall so many movie scenes of a character holding onto her bed frame, gasping as she's laced tighter and tighter into an uncomfortable, constricting garment. But corsets today, when made to fit, can be comfortable, supportive garments that also provide smoothing and reduction where you want it. They can help distribute the weight of the hoop skirt and petticoats, preventing discomfort from digging waistbands. And for cosplayers, they can provide a sturdy, structural piece around the chest for securing fantastical elements, like extra limbs, robot prosthetics, ghostly chains, or pounds of glittering gems.

At a very basic level, corsets work through a combination of fabric and boning to create structure. The fabric is cut into specific shapes that when sewn together create 3-dimensional shape and tension as it wraps around your body. The boning keeps the fabric pulled taut vertically, preventing it from collapsing or bunching where it might otherwise collapse. Because the fabric and boning are both in tension while on the body—especially if the corset is reducing the waist or supporting a larger bust—it's extremely important to use a pattern that is adjusted to your measurements, and good-quality materials. This is even more important if you're planning on making a corset that will be worn as an undergarment and reused in the future.

COSPLAYER: Cowbutt Crunchies

COSTUME: Princess Bubblegum from *Adventure Time* (original design)

Photo by Sorairo Days

COSPLAYER: Dresses and Capes

COSTUME: Sally from *The Nightmare Before Christmas* (original design)

Photo by Legendofsach

Corsetry, as a specialty, can be overwhelming for cosplayers just dipping their toes into the cosplay world. There are so many choices and decisions to make! Historical versus modern, how much to reduce, busk or no busk, choosing materials, how to use boning and where to put them, how many layers, boning materials, cups versus overbust versus underbust … the list goes on!

When approaching the corsetry topic in terms of ballgown creation, we break down the decisions very broadly:

- Is it better to wear a corset as an undergarment, with an exterior bodice, or can the corset serve as the bodice? Is there extreme ornamentation on the design that needs to be mounted to structural support? Are there future costumes that would also benefit from a reusable undergarment?

- Is there a specific time period the costume is referencing? Is there a specific silhouette? Is the character and design extremely curvy with an hourglass figure, or do they have a flattened front? What is the core shape the corset is creating?

Once you have a clearer idea of your end goal, you can search for a suitable pattern. While drafting your own corset is certainly possible, corsets are extremely fiddly garments, and very small changes can change the fit in extreme ways. It is almost always easier to start with a base pattern and resize as needed. Additionally, if you're looking to replicate a specific historical style—a Victorian corset, regency-style stays, a modern cupped fashion corset—buying the matching pattern style sets you up for success. See Resources and Supplies (page 127) for corset pattern sources.

CORSET CONSTRUCTION

Because corset construction is very dependent on a particular pattern, style, fabrics, method of boning, and corset maker's preferences, specific construction instructions are difficult to provide. Instead, we've included general suggestions, tips, and tricks for you to keep in mind as your follow the pattern instructions or your own favorite methods of construction.

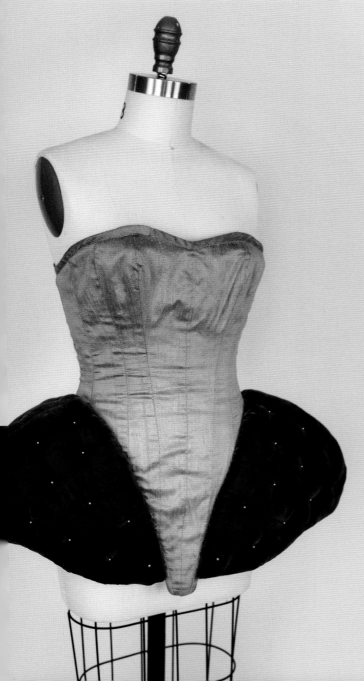

Fabric Selection

Just as using quality boning (page 22) is incredibly important for building a good structure, so is using at least one layer that is made with a strong fabric that has little to no stretch. Sewists who make corsets regularly often invest in coutil, a specialty fabric designed specifically for making corsets (page 26). It has no stretch at all, but a heavy cotton duck or a tightly woven twill also works well for cosplay.

If you intend your corset to be an undergarment, you can certainly get away with a single layer of sturdy fabric for strength and boning channels for structure, and be finished!

Alternatively, if your corset is a visible part of your costume, you almost certainly need more layers. Multiple layers include the same fashion fabric as the rest of your gown (or a contrasting bodice fabric if that is the plan), and a strength layer, at minimum.

Tip

While not strictly required, we recommend lining your corset for comfort. A medium-weight cotton in a complementary color is a great choice.

Determining Your Size

Consult the pattern sizing not just for your waist, but for bust and hip measurements as well. It's extremely common to be different sizes at different points of your body. If you find you are one size at the bust and another at the waist, you can use a ruler and pen to gently draw a transition line between the two sizes directly on the pattern to create new cutting lines.

Cutting the Fabric

You need to cut a full set of patterns for every layer of fabric. So, if you have a fashion fabric, a strength layer, and a lining, cut the full set of pattern pieces three times.

Fabric Cutting Tips

- Cut the corset panels individually, instead of stacking the fabric to cut. This prevents fabric from shifting and ensures that each panel is exact.

- Label the pattern pieces. Many patterns have between 10 and 12 panels, some of which can look very similar. Label all the notches and which direction is the top on each piece as well—it's easier than you think to accidentally sew something upside down or inside out!

Sewing the Panels

There are several ways to sew the corset panels together, depending on the desired result. Remember, for an undergarment corset, you only need the strength fabric, but a lining is a nice addition for comfort and durability for both an undergarment corset and an outer garment corset.

If the stitching for the boning channels will be visible on the finished corset, lay out all the pieces of strength fabric with the matching fashion fabric piece. Baste the pieces with wrong sides together along all four edges to prevent them from shifting when you sew them together. These pieces should now be treated as one for the rest of the corset construction.

If you prefer the boning channels to not show on the finished corset, they can be hidden by treating the fashion, strength, and lining layers completely separately during assembly, and attaching boning channels only to the strength layer. In this case the fashion fabric layer is attached after the lining is installed (page 44).

- If your corset doesn't have a center front opening, pin together the corset panels and stitch. It's generally best to pin and sew one seam at a time. Once all the panels are stitched, press open the seam allowances—this reduces bulk if you install any boning over the seam or allowance.

- If your corset has a functional front opening, you'll need to install a two-piece busk. Installing a busk is an involved process, but it is certainly an option for ambitious makers. It is not covered in this book, but commercial pattern instructions have good installation instructions.

- Set the pieced corset aside and assemble the strength (if not basted to the fabric) and lining pieces, following the same steps.

Planning for Boning

It is important to plan for boning placement before you start sewing. Choosing where to put your boning is dependent on several things: the overall size of the corset, the level of structure needed, the curviness of the corset, and personal preference. Once you decide where you want to install boning, refer to Installing Boning (page 40).

For a boned corset with a center back opening

Generally, you should support each seam with at least one piece of boning. Use the assembly seams to help determine bone placement. You can apply the boning along one or both sides of the seams. Plan to apply boning on both sides of the seams that need more struc-ture, like those on either side of the front and front-middle panels. Pay attention to the shape of the corset where you plan to use boning—if the boning needs to follow complex curves, you should use spiral steel. For areas where the boning is applied in a straight up-and-down direction—for example on the center front—straight steel is a good choice.

For boning placement on the center back edge, measure in ⅝″ from the open back edges to allow room to attach the lining. This is placement for the first center back bone. Then measure in another ½″ (to allow for lacing holes) before marking for any additional back bones. Straight steel is the very best boning for along the center back, even for corsets which have plastic or alternative boning everywhere else.

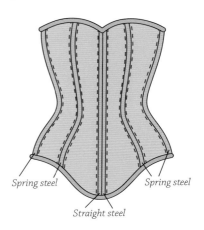

Spring steel   Spring steel

Straight steel

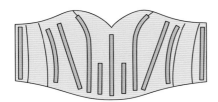

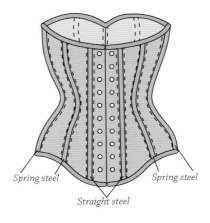

Spring steel   Spring steel

Straight steel

Note

If there is a center front opening, you'll need to install a busk, which replaces the three front bones.

You are always welcome to add more boning. Boning should generally be oriented vertically, and long enough to pro-vide tension along most of the length of the panel to which it is applied. If you're not sure whether to add more boning or not, even an unfinished corset can be tried on to check for areas where the fabric tends to crumple or creates horizontal wrinkles, which are signs that more tension is needed. If you are especially curvy or plus size, you may find adding more boning around areas of support to be helpful. Some historical styles of corsets (also called *stays*) call for dense, tightly packed boning to achieve conical or other less natural shapes.

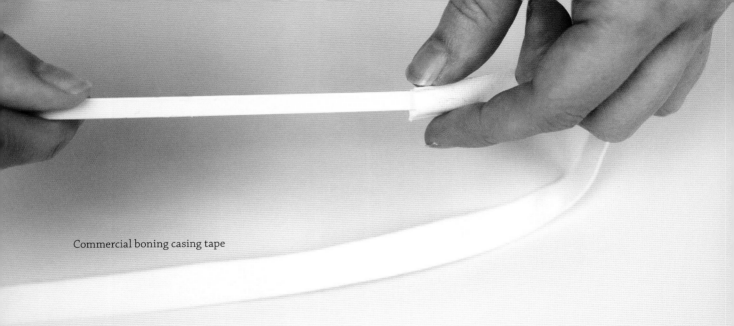

Commercial boning casing tape

Installing Boning

Generally, we prefer to purchase commercial boning casing tape (available from any specialty supplier) to save time and make installation simpler; however, you can also make your own casing tape which works just as well (see How to Make Boning Casing Tape, page 43).

There are two ways to install the boning:

- With boning casing tape that forms channels for the boning. We prefer this method as it allows us to arrange and install our boning channels much earlier in the construction process. This is especially useful for bodice-style, outer-garment corsets which are often heavily embellished, which would need to be done before adding the lining.

- Or by assembling more of the corset, including attaching the lining. Then stitch parallel lines through the strength and lining layer to create channels between the two layers. Slide the bones into the channels.

Whichever method you use to install the boning, make sure you have snug channels to prevent the boning from wiggling and shifting.

With Boning Casing Tape

Once you have sewn the panels together and have a plan for where to add boning, use a ruler and chalk or a fabric pen to mark any channels not aligned with an existing seam. This helps prevent crooked installation.

1. Cut boning casing tape into strips. Measure placement marks and seams where boning will be applied—they all might be slightly different based on location and curve. Cut strips ½″ shorter than measurements.

2. Center boning casing tape, or casing tape you've made yourself (page 43), over marked placement lines and/or vertical seams, with the cut ends of the casing tape at least ¼″ away from the top and bottom edges. Make sure both the fabric and tape are smooth and that the tape follows seam contours.

3. Sew the boning casing in place. Line up the sewing machine needle at the very edge of the channel, ideally just ⅛" (or a hair less) away from the edge. Stitch all the way down the casing tape, across the open bottom of the casing, and back up the other side. Take your time and check periodically that the base corset layer and tape are smooth against each other.

4. Repeat to create boning channels to hold boning wherever desired.

5. Measure each channel and subtract ½". Channels are often different lengths. Use the measurements to cut the boning itself (page 23).

6. Finish both ends of the boning (page 23) before sliding it completely into the channel. Push the boning pieces completely into the casings.

Tip

When inserting the boning pieces, make sure they are not in the way of finishing the top and bottom edges or adding embellishments to the finished edges. There should be at least ½" clearance at the top and bottom edges to sew without hitting the boning.

7. Before sealing the top channel edges, try the unfinished corset on to ensure no additional boning is needed. A friend or family member can hold the corset on you, applying some tension, or you can temporarily baste corset lacing tape to the back panels to give yourself temporary lacing holes to conduct your own test fit.

8. If your corset is strictly a utilitarian undergarment, and you're happy with the amount of boning you have, you can use machine or hand stitching to close the channels at the top.

COSPLAYER: Kaye Cosplay

COSTUME: Carlotta from *The Phantom of the Opera*

Photo by Amie Photos

9. If you are making a boned bodice or lined corset, add the lining now.

Tip

Adding Embellishments

If you plan to machine stitch embellishments—trim, appliqué, or other elements—in place, you should do so before installing the boning. Be sure to stop stitching when you arrive at a channel, skip over it, and continue stitching on the other side of the channel. *Never* machine stitch over a piece of boning—your needle could break and damage your machine, or hurt you.

If you plan to hand stitch your embellishments in place, you can apply them before or after the boning is installed.

How to Make Boning Casing Tape

Instead of buying pre-made casing tape, you can easily and affordably make your own using strong, non-stretch corset fabric like coutil or twill. To determine how much you need, measure from the top to the bottom of the corset and multiply this number by the number of bones you plan to install, adding a few inches for contingency.

1. Make one continuous strip or cut fabric into long strips equal to the determined measurement. Cut the strip (or strips) parallel to the selvage on the lengthwise grain. If you are using ¼″-wide bones, cut the fabric strips 1½″ wide to make a ½″ total finished casing width.

2. Fold the strips in half lengthwise and press. If abric has a wrong side, fold wrong sides together. Sew the raw edges together with a ¼″ seam allowance.

3. Manipulate the strip so the seam is centered on top. Press the seam allowance open and trim any excess that can be seen from the other side of casing.

4. Test-fit a piece of boning by inserting it into the casing tape. It should fit somewhat loosely at this point since some slack will disappear when the tape is sewn in place.

5. Follow same steps as for purchased boning tape to create boning channels.

Completing the Corset

For a corset with a center back opening

1. With all channels created, boning installed, and any machine embellishments attached, it's time to attach the lining.

Pin the corset layers with right sides together, with the seams aligned. Pin near the seams and along the back openings. Sew the back openings only with a ½˝ seam allowance, then turn corset right side out so the wrong sides are together. Press the back seams.

2. Stitch ⅜˝ from the top edge to secure corset and lining together and close the tops of the bone casings. Sew slowly in case any bones have slid upwards in their channels. Since the bottom channels were sealed shut when casings were applied, you can simply hand baste the corset and lining together. Don't worry about raw edges for now, but you can trim the top and bottom seam allowances to neaten them up.

3. Once the layers are secured, use purchased ½˝-wide double-fold bias tape to encase the raw edges. Unfold the bias tape and with right sides together, sew the bias tape to the top edge of the corset, ⅜˝ from the edge. Fold the bias tape over the top edge and hand sew the folded edge of the bias tape to the inside of the corset.

Tip

The bias tape can be the same or a different color from the rest of your corset. You can choose fun contrasting fabrics for the binding since the binding is not structural. Your imagination is the limit!

4. Measure and mark grommet placements (see Center Back Laced Closing. Install grommets, following the manufacturer's instructions.

Making Your Own Bias Tape

While bias tape is commercially available in lots of colors, making your own can give you a perfect match for corset finishing.

1. Using a woven fabric, carefully mark 2˝-wide bias strips on a 45° angle from the selvage edge of the fabric. Cut 2 strips, to equal the circumference of the corset top and bottom edges, respectively. Depending on size, you'll need ¾ to 1½ yards of fabric.

2. Fold each strip in half lengthwise and press. Bring the raw edges to the center, crease, and press again. This method creates ½˝-wide bias, perfect for binding a corset.

If you used a stretchy or non-woven fabric for your fashion fabric, or would like to use it as binding, simply cut the 2˝-wide strips along the direction of the fabric that has the most stretch! This can be a bit more difficult to install than traditional woven bias tape so it might be easier to secure it by hand.

Center Back Laced Closing

Once the top and bottom edges of your corset are bound, the only thing left is to create the lacing holes in order to pull the corset closed.

While you can hand stitch to finish the edges of the lacing holes, which is always a nice detail on historically accurate garments, you can also use 2-part grommets to secure the holes. Grommets are relatively quick and easy to apply, and are relatively secure, unlike single-part eyelets, which we don't recommend for corsetry, as they tend to pop out!

You will need:

- an awl
- grommets, size 00 (hole diameter $^5/_{32}$″) or size 0 (hole diameter ¼″)
- 6–10 yards of corset lacing, depending on the number of grommets

Tip

Grommet Size

Make sure to account for the width of your grommets. They have a flange, so the minimum distance between the holes should be large enough that the grommet edges don't touch or overlap. If you use corset size 0 or 00 grommets, you'll need at least ½″ between the centers of holes.

1. Use a ruler to carefully mark placement for the grommets. Generally, the more grommets you have, the more control you will have over the tension of the corset and the more evenly distributed the tension will be. We usually aim for about 1″ between the marks, with first and last grommet installed right below and above the bias binding.

Depending on the corset length, you might need to slightly increase or decrease the distance between grommets to get an even distribution. For corsets with additional cinching at the waist, you may wish to space these center grommets closer together, in order to better handle the extra stress. For additional guidance, consult the placement guide in your corset pattern.

Tip

Determining Distance Between Holes

The easiest way to determine even distribution is to measure the length of the corset between the edges of the bias binding.

Assuming you will space the center of each hole at around an inch apart, and accounting for a buffer between the first grommet and the actual edge of the bias tape, you will always have one fewer holes than the total number of inches of length.

For example, for a corset that is 12¾″ long from edge of bias to bias, 12 - 1 is 11 holes. Divide the remaining excess length, ¾″, by 12, which equals .062, which is the same as $^1/_{16}$″. This means you should install 11 holes, 1$^1/_{16}$″ apart, starting by measuring 1$^1/_{16}$″ from the bias edge. If your excess doesn't divide perfectly evenly, remember this is an approximation; having the second-to-last grommet ⅛″ off truly won't be noticeable.

2. Once the placement is marked, use an awl to carefully make a hole at each mark through all the corset layers. An awl works by pushing threads aside around it as opposed to cutting through them, which helps the longevity of your corset since the fabric does not become compromised. You can use a hole punch or a pair of tiny scissors to cut holes if you don't have an awl but be sure to use a fray block on the holes prior to installing the grommets so the tension does not cause further tearing of the fabric.

3. Install grommets according to the manufacturer's instructions. Generally, the 2 parts are fitted together on either side of the fabric layers and hammered into place with a setting tool. Make sure you install them snugly; loose grommets will fall out over time as you lace and unlace your corset.

4. You can lace the corset from the top downward, or from the bottom up. The direction depends on whether you want more support at the top or the bottom of the corset; try both ways to see what feels better with your corset and your body.

* As you lace, cross the lacing cord over the middle gap and through the next grommet on the opposite side. Be consistent with direction as you thread the cord through the grommets, whether from front to back or from back to front, to prevent laces from tangling.

* When you arrive at the grommet closest to your natural waist, instead of crossing again, thread the lacing cord through the next grommet up or down on same side of the corset. Leave a little slack, then resume the criss-cross lacing for rest of the corset.

- Tie the ends of the cords together with a double bow to keep them secure.

- When you put the corset on, use the vertical loops you created at your waist to pull out all the slack in the laces for a firm fit. You can then tie the two loops in a bow to secure them.

Note: Pre-lacing Your Corset

You can pre-lace your corset before wearing it but be sure to leave lots of slack between the grommets, so the back edges are at least 12˝–15˝ apart. Don't tie the ends of the laces yet—instead put the corset on backwards, so the lacing is situated at your front. Use the loose ends of the laces (not the middle loops) to pull out enough slack so that the corset is not tight or fitted but is not hanging off of you completely. Then tie the loose ends and turn the corset around your body so the laces are in the back. Reach behind yourself and pull out the remainder of the slack of the lace using the middle loops as described above.

This a good option if you don't have a friend or second set of hands to fully lace your corset.

BONED BODICES

Some ballgown bodices benefit from boning, particularly if you won't be wearing a corset as an undergarment. Typically, adding boning to bodices is more for structure than waist reduction or bust support so fewer channels are needed. We usually only install boning along the seamlines. The intention here is to simply prevent buckling. The boning should be installed after the bodice is assembled, but before the lining has been attached. There is not usually a strength fabric layer in boned bodices.

If your fashion material is delicate, or it tends to pull or otherwise show stitching, you may want to apply bones to the bodice lining, which is typically a sturdy cotton fabric. You can also mix shorter and longer pieces of boning as needed, since shorter bones do not carry as much tension as they would in a full corset. See Installing Boning, page 40.

Hoop Skirts

Cosplay gowns come in many shapes and sizes—flowy, delicate skirts that drape around a petticoat, elegant column dresses with empire waists—but none are more iconic than the classic, poufy, princess-style ballgown, with skirts so immense that narrow doors become a problem. And for this style of ballgown, a hoop skirt is an absolute must. Hoop skirts—and their siblings: farthingales, bustles, as well as distant cousin, panniers—are underskirts whose defining features are large, circular bands, or hoops, of rigid material, often steel.

Because hoop skirts are so structured, they are good choices where large amounts of outward volume are desired. The hoop structure requires less fabric than trying to build the equivalent amount of volume from petticoats, and tends to be more comfortable, since it floats away from the body and doesn't trap heat.

If your skirt calls for a circumference of 120″ or more, a hoop skirt might be a good solution. However, because they are so structured, if you want your gown to have a draped or "swishy" feel to it, you may need to look at other options for volume. Skirts that are thin throughout the hip and thigh area with more volume at the lower half are also not great candidates for a hoop. Consult your master plan and sources as you decide!

Hoop skirts are generally considered historical garments and were part of everyday fashion, spanning across many time periods, so there is a lot of variation in sizes and shapes. Cosplayers have plenty of inspiration to draw on! The changes in styles across history also mean there's plenty of variation in how a hoop skirt is constructed: Some are solid cloth underskirts with long channels for hoops, some are open-air cages of tape and uncovered steel hoops; some are round, others are elliptical. Cosplayers aiming for a specific historical look and feel to their costume or those aiming for a costume from a period drama may want to check the specific size and shape of hoop skirt in fashion at that time for the most realistic feel.

TYPES OF HOOP SKIRTS

Hoops, regardless of their shape, all work approximately the same way—steel bands provide tension, and their placement and size create the shape of the hoop skirt. The hoops hang in a shape, held off the body by the size of the hoops, and the fabric portion of the skirt keeps them aligned in place vertically. When the weight of petticoats and skirts is applied, the tension of the hoops helps them keep their shape and the entire garment takes on the shape of the hoop skirt. Depending on how far you increase each successive hoop, and how far down the skirt you do so, you can customize the shape of your understructure.

COSPLAYER: Alchemical Cosplay

COSTUME: Astrologian from *Final Fantasy XIV*

Photo by Alexandra Lee Studios

Circular hoop skirts can be made in a variety of shapes. One of the most popular hoop skirts, the A-line hoop skirt, features hoops that are distributed evenly up and down, while growing in circumference at regular intervals. Alternatively, placing more hoops closer together at the top creates a bell-shaped hoop. For instructions to make a simple A-line hoop skirt see How to Make a Circular A-Line Hoop Skirt (page 51)..

A ballgown over a modest bell-shaped hoop skirt

The same gown over a larger A-line hoop skirt

Open hoop skirts feature hoops that don't circle completely around the body but are secured at other points in the skirt. You still must maintain the circular tension of the steel bones because hoop steel naturally wants to flatten. You need to maintain the desired shape, but the open panel in the front doesn't provide any structure to help keep the hoops closed. The same applies to elliptical hoop skirts and other boned underskirts like bustles or panniers; they often use ribbon or fabric panels to complete the circle in such a way as to keep the steel taut.

For our Seraphim outfit, we heavily reinforced the open edges with rigid wire, which we also secured to the hoops. We added heavy wire into the bottom hem that could be bent to the right shape as extra help to maintain the circular shape throughout the rest of the undergarment. If your costume calls for an open hoop, consider how you'll engineer tension back into your skirt.

COSPLAYER: Cowbutt Crunchies
COSTUME: Seraphim from Sakizo
Photo by Alexandra Lee Studios

Make or Buy a Hoop Skirt

Hoop skirts can be built or bought, depending on the need. While purchased hoops work, we always encourage cosplayers to build their own. You can certainly use commercial patterns. They are available online and are relatively inexpensive; however, drafting and building your own hoop skirt is quite straightforward.

Tip

Whether you make your own, or buy a hoop skirt, avoid plastic hooping since it is too weak for hoop skirts. Even thinner steel bone hoops can collapse.

Designing your own hoop skirt allows you to build in adjustability, so you can use one hoop skirt for many costumes of different sizes and shapes.

Building your own hoop skirt allows you to use proper, heavy hoop steel. This means your skirt can hold the weight of large or multiple petticoats and not collapse under even the most elaborate, over embellished skirts. Quality materials also last longer; we've used the same hoop skirts for years, across dozens of costumes. Purchased hoop skirts often use much thinner steel, or even plastic hooping, and thin polyester fabric.

Thin 6mm versus heavier 10mm hoopsteel

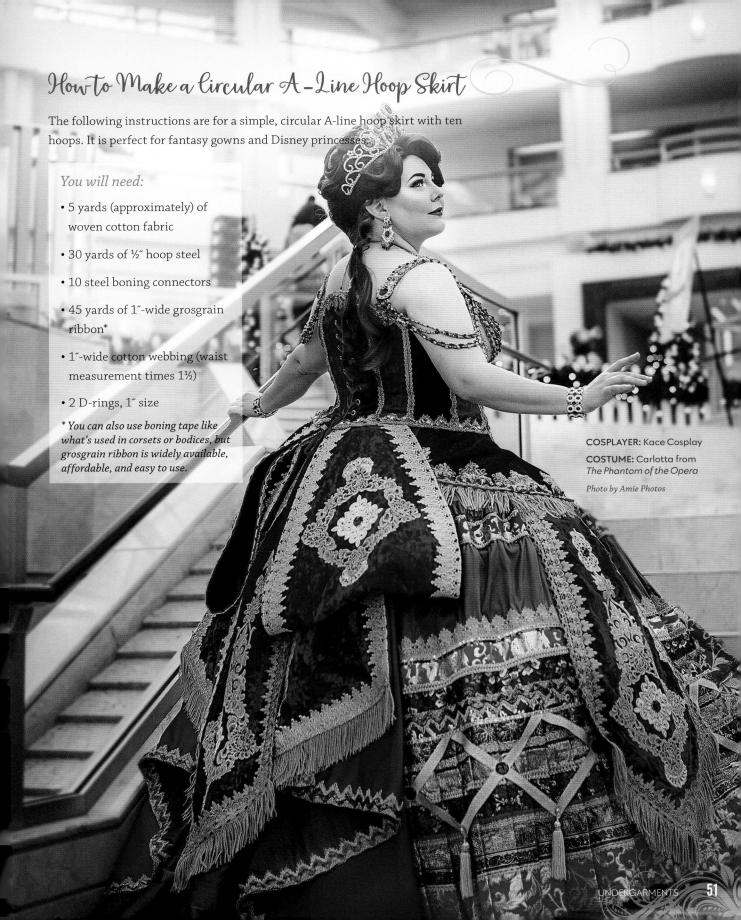

How to Make a Circular A-Line Hoop Skirt

The following instructions are for a simple, circular A-line hoop skirt with ten hoops. It is perfect for fantasy gowns and Disney princesses.

You will need:

- 5 yards (approximately) of woven cotton fabric

- 30 yards of ½″ hoop steel

- 10 steel boning connectors

- 45 yards of 1″-wide grosgrain ribbon*

- 1″-wide cotton webbing (waist measurement times 1½)

- 2 D-rings, 1″ size

* You can also use boning tape like what's used in corsets or bodices, but grosgrain ribbon is widely available, affordable, and easy to use.

COSPLAYER: Kace Cosplay

COSTUME: Carlotta from *The Phantom of the Opera*

Photo by Amie Photos

PLAN THE LENGTH AND CIRCUMFERENCE

You need the following measurements: waist circumference, length from waist to floor, and intended bottom circumference.

While your planned hoop circumference depends on your costume and proportions plan, as a visual reference, a medium-sized hoop is around 125″ in circumference and is the common size seen with historical reenactment. Smaller hoops are commonly available as bridal garments online, and large hoops, the kind you really only see in extreme costuming and cosplay, can get as large as 150″–170″ in circumference.

Tip

The Value of an Adjustable Hoop Skirt

If you hope to use your hoop skirt for more than one costume, you can adjust a larger hoop skirt for a smaller costume, but you can't adjust a small hoop skirt to make it larger without taking it apart and adding new steel.

While the exact measurements of each hoop depend on how large you want your largest hoop, and whether your hoop skirt will be mostly one shape, or adjustable between A-line and bell shapes, the average largish hoop skirt will need around 30 yards of steel, which is no small amount! This is why making your skirt adjustable pays off—both in cost and effort.

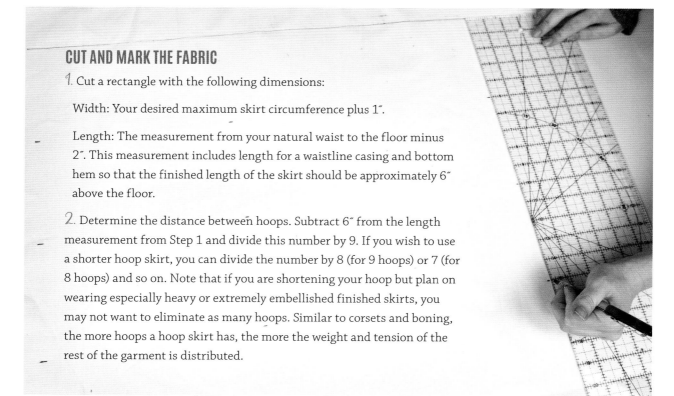

CUT AND MARK THE FABRIC

1. Cut a rectangle with the following dimensions:

   Width: Your desired maximum skirt circumference plus 1″.

   Length: The measurement from your natural waist to the floor minus 2″. This measurement includes length for a waistline casing and bottom hem so that the finished length of the skirt should be approximately 6″ above the floor.

2. Determine the distance between hoops. Subtract 6″ from the length measurement from Step 1 and divide this number by 9. If you wish to use a shorter hoop skirt, you can divide the number by 8 (for 9 hoops) or 7 (for 8 hoops) and so on. Note that if you are shortening your hoop but plan on wearing especially heavy or extremely embellished finished skirts, you may not want to eliminate as many hoops. Similar to corsets and boning, the more hoops a hoop skirt has, the more the weight and tension of the rest of the garment is distributed.

3. Lay the fabric flat with the wrong side up and measure and mark the hoop placement along the short edges, as well as at points across the fabric width. Use chalk or a fabric pen. Allow room at the top edge for the waistline casing and at the bottom for the hem. From the top, measure down 2½″ and mark the waistline casing. From the bottom, measure up 1½″ and mark the hemline. Measuring down from the waistline casing line, mark for boning placement as determined in Step 2. It is helpful to use a ruler or yardstick to draw in placement markings across the fabric.

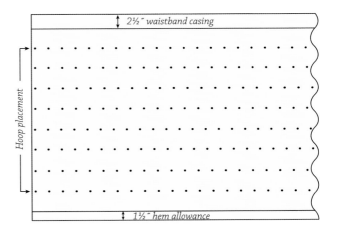

MAKE THE HOOP CHANNELS AND FINISH THE SKIRT

1. Cut 10 lengths (or the number of desired hoops) of grosgrain ribbon equal to width/circumference measurement from Step 1, minus 4″. Use a match to seal the ribbon edges. The ribbon channels do not overlap (or even meet) so that you can access the steel hoops later to adjust their length as needed for future costumes. Center and pin the ribbon pieces over the hoop placement marks.

2. Sew each of the ribbon pieces in place, stitching no more than ⅛″ away from the ribbon edges.

Tip

Hoop channels should be snug enough to hold the steel but loose enough so the skirt can be adjusted around the steel. Hoop channels should be looser than the channels used in corset making.

3. With the right sides of the fabric together and the ribbon channels on the inside, sew the short sides with a ½″ seam allowance. Stop sewing at the marked waistband line. This is the center back seam. Make sure the seam does not catch the openings of the ribbon channels. Press open.

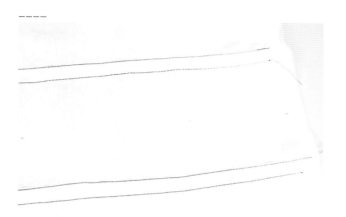

4. Fold and press the top and bottom edges ½″ to the wrong side.

5. At the bottom edge, fold the pressed fold to the wrong side again so it meets the marked hemline. It should almost, but not quite, touch the bottom edge of the last piece of ribbon. Stitch the hem, leaving an unstitched portion of 1½″ on either side of the center back seam. This creates the last boning channel.

6. At the top edge, fold to the wrong side again so the fold meets the waistline casing marking. Sew along the inside pressed fold to create a casing. Attach the D-rings to one end of webbing to create an adjustable closure. Insert the webbing into the casing.

7. Now it's time to measure to determine the hoopsteel lengths needed to create the A-line shape.

Bottom hoop—Measure the fabric circumference and add 2″ for overlap. Note that the bottom 2 hoops—for the bottom channel and the hem allowance—should be cut to the same length and treated as a single hoop.

Top hoop—Because it's so close to your waist, there is a minimum size for the top hoop. The easiest way to find that size is to take your waist measurement and divide it by 6.28. Add the amount of the distance between hoops that you calculated in Step 2. Multiply the total by 6.28 to find the minimum size. You might also want to try the skirt on and feed different amounts of hoopsteel (without cutting it) into the top channel. Play around with the length until you're happy with the overall size and shape it creates around your hips. Mark that length and cut with 2″ excess for overlap.

Now that you have a maximum length for the bottom hoop and a minimum length for the top hoop, you can figure out the measurements of the other eight: [The largest hoop length] minus [the smallest hoop length] divided by [the number of hoops minus 1] equals the hoop step-up length. For example, if you are using 9 hoops, divide by 8. So if your top hoop is 60″ and your bottom is 160″, your step up would be (160 - 60)/8 = 12½″.

For hoop 2: Add the length of the smallest hoop plus the step-up length.

For hoop 3: Add the length of hoop 2 plus the step-up length.

Continue so each hoop increases the same distance from the one above.

8. Cut the hoopsteel (page 23) into the determined measurements and apply boning tips (page 23) over each cut edge.

9. Feed each piece of hoopsteel through its corresponding ribbon channel, pushing the excess skirt fabric so you have plenty of hoopsteel poking out to work with. The hoop should overlap itself by about 2˝. Clamp the connectors around the overlapped section to connect the ends. Finished!

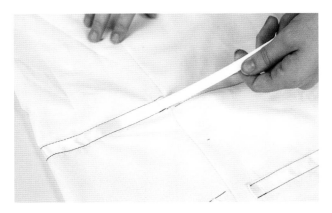

Make the Hoop Skirt Adjustable

To create adjustable hoop lengths, we like to use special hoop connectors that clamp around where the steel overlaps itself. The key to these is not to clamp *too* tightly, or you won't be able to adjust it later to make the hoops smaller. After carefully easing the tipped steel into the channel until it's a smooth circle, tighten the clamp just enough that the steel is not loose but can still be moved through the channel with some effort. Then carefully ease the clamped steel into the channel until it's a smooth circle. Remember, hoop channels are not as snug as corset channels.

When you want to decrease the size of a hoop, pull the hoop out through the gap in the ribbon. Adjusting the hoop size will create an extra tail of steel that extends; you can use small rubber bands or even sturdy tape to keep it snug against the ring.

WEARING A HOOP SKIRT

An extremely important thing to keep in mind is that a hoop skirt should never be your only undergarment; it almost always requires petticoats! This is because of the way the hoop skirt works—the hoops provide the structure, and any skirt fabric will cover the hoops but also drape and sink in between them. It gives your final dress a ribbed effect around the skirt and can ruin the elegant look of an otherwise gorgeous dress. A petticoat provides layering between the hoop and the skirt, giving you smooth, elegant lines.

Petticoats can also be used to adjust the shape of your hoop skirt. If your hoop is a little too small at its maxed-out size or is a cone when you want a bell shape, you can use petticoats to pad it out to its final shape. For some of our largest costumes, we've started with our hoop at its maxed-out size and added three additional petticoats to get the ultimate pouf—so feel free to experiment to nail that perfect cosplay!

Petticoats

Giant, fluffy petticoats serve as both an alternative to a hoop skirt and a complementary undergarment. When worn alone in place of a hoop skirt, a petticoat provides an extra swish of movement that's perfect for posing, dancing, and twirling. Petticoats are less rigid and cumbersome than hoop skirts but sacrifice size in exchange. They're generally smaller and more likely to be crushed down under the weight of a heavy skirt and are best paired with small to moderate-size lightweight gowns.

For larger gowns that require a hoop skirt, a petticoat is still a must, in order to smooth out the bumpy bones of the hoop and hide any unsightly lines that might show through the outer skirt fabric. There are exceptions, of course, such as slim, fitted sheath dresses, but a petticoat of some kind will almost always improve your cosplay. Making a petticoat is a beginner-friendly sewing project, and the same petticoat can be reused many times for costumes with similar silhouettes. So, investing in making the perfect petti is time well spent.

A hoop skirt capped with a petticoat for added volume and softness

FABRIC, SHAPE, AND VOLUME

As you plan your ballgown, ask yourself a few questions about the desired volume and shape.

How large do I want my gown to be?

A petticoat will fill out a small to moderate-size gown, but a larger ballgown will require a petticoat layered over a hoop skirt.

What shape do I want my gown to have?

Skip ahead to Skirt Shapes (page 73) and choose between a conical A-line or a cupcake shape that requires additional volume at the top. The shape of the skirt impacts the shape and construction of the petticoat.

Is my hoop skirt already my desired shape?

If not, create a petticoat that will add volume in the desired areas.

Once you know what you need your petticoat to do—whether that is just adding some soft padding over your perfectly shaped hoop or completely filling the bottom of a flowy A-line skirt—you can choose the three major factors that create a petticoat: fabrics, shape, and volume.

COSPLAYER: Cowbutt Crunchies
COSTUME: Deku Princess from *The Legend of Zelda* (original design)
Photo by Sorairo Days

Fabrics

Cosplay petticoats are typically created from one of two types of fabrics: netting and organza. Both of these fabrics are easy to find, relatively affordable, and easy to work with, and both produce good volume. However, historical costumers may turn to different materials, such as cotton and other natural fibers, or traditional petticoat crinoline.

Netting

Netting is a sheer textile with the yarns of thread looped or knotted only at their intersections, creating open spaces between the yarns. It is both lighter and stiffer than organza. While netting looks very similar to tulle, and is made in a similar way, tulle is a finer fabric that will not provide the same amount of volume. Don't confuse either of these fabrics with "mesh," which is sometimes sold as "bridal" or "illusion" netting. Look for a netting fabric that has larger spaces, is made of nylon or polyester, and has a stiff or crisp texture. Because netting is so stiff, it's an excellent choice for building volume fast.

We often use netting for single- or two-tier petticoats that are designed to go over a hoop, since the stiffness of the fabric smooths over and easily hides the hoop ridges. It can also hold up to heavier skirt fabrics like duchess satin or upholstery weights. However, if your skirt is made of a delicate fabric with more drape, the stiff peaks and gathers of netting might show through. In these cases, choose an organza petticoat or a combination of two petticoats: a netting petti for volume with an organza petti on top for smoothing.

Organza

Organza is a woven fabric that is semi-sheer with a slight sheen and has great body when gathered. Organza is found in many different fiber contents, including high-end, beautiful silk organza. For a cosplay petticoat, however, we recommend basic polyester organza; it's hard-wearing, easy to clean, and affordable in large amounts of yardage. Organza is a great option for multi-tier or short (knee-length) petticoats since it still drapes at short lengths, unlike netting which can be too stiff for knee-length skirts.

Shape

The shape of a petticoat is created by its number and length of tiers. A tier is a rectangle of fabric which has been gathered on one side in order to reduce its width. Each time you add a tier, the volume of the petticoat increases at the area at which you added the tier, and thus affects the shape. A petticoat can be a single tier, which would be a single row of fabric, cut to the height of the entire skirt, gathered at the waist. Or it could be four or five tiers that balloon outward at each tier seam, resulting in a conical A-line petticoat. When worn alone (without a hoop skirt), the shape of that petticoat will be what creates the overall silhouette of your skirt.

Single Tier   *Two Tiers*   *Four Tiers*

If you plan to wear a petticoat over a hoop skirt, a petti with fewer tiers adds smoothing and body without severely altering the silhouette of the hoop. The simplest version of this is a single tier of organza, gathered at the waist. For a single-tier petticoat designed to smooth over a hoop skirt, we recommend stacking 2 to 3 layers of material for extra volume.

Alternatively, using a 2-tier petticoat with one long top tier and one short (10″–15″ long) gathered tier at the bottom can add an extra, fluffy kick to heavier or larger skirts!

Volume

While the tier structure affects a petticoat's shape, the number of layers is what determines the overall volume and size. Additional layers will push the topmost ones outward, similar to the layers of an onion, which get bigger with each layer. You can create a single-tier, 10-layer petticoat that is massive, or a four-tier petticoat with a single layer that provides very little pouf.

COSPLAYER:
Cowbutt Crunchies

COSTUME: Marceline
from *Adventure Time*
(original design)

Photo by Amie Photos

How To Build a 4-Tier Petticoat

The following instructions are for a medium-volume, A-line, organza petticoat which can be worn either by itself under a circle skirt or A-line dress, or layered over a hoop skirt to add additional mass and bottom floof. While these instructions are for 4 tiers, once you understand the basic steps you can adjust the measurements, number of tiers, and other factors to build any kind of tiered petticoat!

MAKE A PLAN

You will need to know the following:

- your hip *or* waist measurement, whichever is larger

- the desired finished circumference of your skirt

- the desired finished length (including hem allowance at the bottommost tier)

Note

Note that if you plan on finishing the bottom edge of your petticoat by serging or binding the edge, no special steps need to be taken. If you would like to do a rolled or double-fold hem, you need to add an additional 1″ to the height of the bottom tier only.

- If you plan to use this petticoat for a very specific costume with an unusual length, consult your costume plan and measurements as discussed in Plan Your Project beginning on page 16.

- If you intend to make a general-use petticoat for many of your ballgown and cosplay needs, take a measurement from your waist to the floor and subtract 3″. If you are a cosplayer who always wears high heels, add 1″–3″ inches back in, depending on your favored heel height. Then, follow the worksheet below to find the dimensions for each tier.

Tier Length and Height Worksheet

Total amounts include 1″ total for ½″ seam allowances.

Length of each tier:

Tier 1: _____ (waist or hip measurement) × 3 = _____ + 1″ = _____

Tier 2: _____ (Tier 1) × 3 = _____ + 1″ = _____

Tier 3: _____ (Tier 2) × 3 = _____ + 1″ = _____

Tier 4: _____ (Tier 3) × 3 = _____ + 1″ = _____

Height of each tier:

_____ (desired total length) divided by 4 = _____ + 1″ = _____

CUT THE FABRIC

Once you determine the dimensions of the tiers, spread out as much of your fabric as possible. Measure and mark each piece with chalk or a fabric marking pen. There are several ways to do this, but we suggest making a template—it's quick, easy, and accurate. To make a template, cut a rectangular piece of poster board or cardboard to same height as the tiers and several feet long. If you are working with tiers of different heights, remember to cut a new template for each tier height.

Use the template as a ruler by aligning one edge with the fabric selvage and the top edge with the top raw edge of the fabric. Mark along the bottom edge in 12″ sections.

As you cut each tier, especially longer ones, label it with the tier number using a fabric marker. Remember to add a hem allowance to the bottom tier if you've decided on a folded hem.

Tip

Finishing Edges and Enclosed Seams

While organza is a wonderful choice for a petticoat due to its structure and weight, it does fray horribly. Since petticoats are hard-wearing undergarments, it's important to address the fraying issue.

If you have a serger, or an overlock function on your sewing machine, you can serge or overlock the organza pieces on all four sides immediately after cutting. You can then sew the rest of your petticoat as directed below.

French seams are a classic method of finishing seams on sheer fabrics.

1. Sew pieces *wrong sides together* with a ½″ seam. Trim the seam allowance to about ¼″.

2. Fold the fabric with *right sides together*, enclosing the first seam allowance, and press.

3. Stitch about ½″ from the folded edge to encase raw edges and create a finished look.

Flat-felled seams are enclosed, and therefore prevent fraying, but the pieces are joined traditionally and then finished.

1. After sewing the pieces *with right sides together*, press the seam allowances open.

2. Trim one side of the seam allowance to about ¼″.

3. Press the entire seam allowance to one side with the wider one over the trimmed one. Then carefully fold the wider seam allowance around the trimmed one, essentially wrapping it.

4. Press and topstitch the folded edge.

SEW THE TIERS

1. Sew each tier. The first tier usually requires only one piece, but other tiers will usually require joining pieces together to reach the desired circumference. Join the pieces as needed by sewing them with right sides together.

2. For first tier, fold the piece in half widthwise and pin the short edges together. Stitch, leaving 2″–3″ open at the top edge for the back opening.

3. Pin and sew the short edges together to make the pieces for each of the tiers.

4. Hem the bottom edge of the bottom tier. You can use a regular hem, or a rolled hem, or leave it unhemmed as long as you have a serged edge and didn't include a hem allowance when you cut the pieces. You can also use ribbon or bias tape to bind the edge if a hem allowance wasn't added—this tends to add extra body to the edge, as well as a fun flash of color or embellishment.

Tip

For extra body, feed fishing line into a rolled hem to produce a lettuce-edge hem. You can even apply a narrow horsehair braid if desired (page 86).

Gathering Methods

There are generally three ways to gather fabric, each with its own set of pros and cons. We usually use the couching method for our petticoats because it is easy to determine how much to gather the larger tier to match the length of the smaller tier.

PINNING

1. Mark the center back, center front, and side points of the bottom tier on the top edge. Mark the same points on both long edges of the next-to-the-bottom tier. A good way to do this is by aligning seams at the center back.

2. With right sides together, nest the upper tier inside the bottom tier. Line up the marks and pin the tiers together. There should be plenty of excess fabric on the bottom tier between the marks. Using a measuring tape, find the midpoint between the two sets of pins on both tiers and then pin those points together. Continue doing so, measuring between each new set of pins until you have pinned all the excess fabric between the tiers.

Pros: Easily adjustable. Since you manually gather and pin the excess fabric, you can adjust the excess fabric to shift it in one direction or the other. Once the pieces are pinned and adjusted so they are evenly distributed, you are ready to sew.

Cons: Extremely time-consuming, especially for super long pieces of fabric. Gathering is generally less even than with the other two methods.

BASTING

1. Set your sewing machine to the longest stitch length possible. On the edge to be gathered, sew ¼˝ from the fabric edge. Sew a second line next to the first, ⅜˝ from the fabric edge. Leave long thread tails at both ends.

2. Remove the fabric from the machine and knot the thread tails together at one end. Hold the thread tails from the other end of the stitching. Holding the threads taut, slide the fabric along the thread, bunching it up and gathering it.

Pros: Very easy. The basting line is nearly invisible after the petticoat is assembled. Easy to ungather if you make piece too tight.

Cons: Difficult to gather to a specific length, so you have to continuously measure as you gather. If the thread breaks, all your gathering comes loose, so can be risky on very long pieces of fabric.

COUCHING

You need a heavy-duty thread or cord, such as cotton crochet thread.

1. Set your sewing machine to a long and wide zigzag stitch. Align the fabric so you are stitching ¼″ from the edge. Center the thread or cord under the presser foot, but on top of the fabric.

2. Stitch so the machine thread zigzags over the thread or cord, trapping it against fabric but not stitching through it.

3. To gather, hold the thread or cord taut and push the fabric along it to gather the fabric, just like sliding a pair of curtains back on a curtain rod.

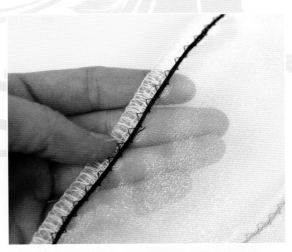

Pros: Very easy to gather to the exact length. You can cut the length of cord to the desired measurement and gather the fabric as you sew, pulling the cord toward you to continue to sew any ungathered areas. The cord is sturdier than sewing thread, so it's less likely to break than with the basting method.

Cons: Time-consuming to apply the couched cord, and to remove it after your petticoat is assembled. Leaves more visible additional stitching on the seam allowances of the tiers once assembled, so it can look messy.

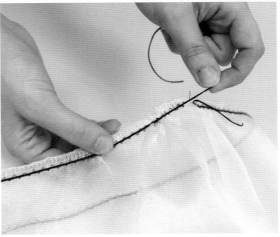

GATHER AND JOIN THE TIERS

1. Gather (page 64) the unhemmed edge of the bottom tier to match the length of the adjacent tier.

2. With right sides together, nest the adjacent tier inside the bottom tier, with edges pinned together. Sew the tiers together, adjusting the gathers as needed. The bottom tier should pouf out a bit where it hangs from the adjacent tier.

3. Repeat the gathering method of choice to connect the remaining tiers. Gather the free edge of the top tier to match your waist measurement.

4. Before adding the waistband, try on the petticoat, with a hoop skirt, if applicable. Consider volume—have you achieved the shape and size you want? Keep in mind that heavy skirt fabric can compress the petticoat down significantly, so it might be a good idea to make it just a little poufier than your final desired size.

5. Once you are happy with the shape and volume of the petticoat, you can move on to the waistband.

Tip

Adding Petticoat Volume

If you want more volume, it's as easy as cutting and gathering more tiers, using the same measurements and instructions as for the original petticoat. You don't necessarily have to create a complete second layer with four tiers, especially if you are only looking for more flare; you can add additional layers starting at any of the tier seams to add volume below that point.

- For a more mermaid-style flare, or extra pouf and body only at the bottom of the petticoat, cut and gather an additional bottom-tier piece and attach it to the same seam that joined the original bottom tier to the one above it.

- For more body throughout, make an extra layer with the second, third, and fourth tiers and sew it to the same seam that joined the original top two tiers.

- Experiment and add partial layers or extra tiers as you choose. However, we advise not connecting more than two gathered tiers to any single-layer tier above it—so if you find you need three pieces of the bottom tier to get the amount of volume you want, you need to attach them to at least two layers of the adjacent tier.

MAKE THE WAISTBAND

We suggest a 2″ finished waistband, which is wide enough to be comfortable and secure, but narrow enough that additional tailoring to fit your waist isn't needed.

1. Use a sturdy, non-stretch fabric like twill or heavy cotton. Cut 1 piece on the fabric grain 5″ wide by your waist measurement + 4″.

2. Press ½″ to the wrong side on each long edge.

3. Fold and press the piece in half lengthwise, with wrong sides together. You should now have a piece long enough to wrap around your waist with a bit of overlap.

Note

As tempting as it is, never use bias tape as a waistband! Bias tape is designed to stretch—definitely not something you want when a snug waistband is what keeps your skirt on!

4. Unfold the waistband and pin a single side to the edge of the top tier, with right sides together. If you have multiple layers for the top tier, treat them all as one piece for this seam. The waistband should extend beyond the center back opening by about 2″ on one side and by ½″ on the other side so that the finished edge of one side lines up with the back opening, and the other side extends beyond the back opening to allow for closures.

5. Sew the waistband to the top tier with a ½″ seam allowance.

6. Fold ½″ to the wrong side on both short ends of the waistband. Refold the waistband and press so seam allowance is pressed into the waistband. Topstitch along the short ends and on the lower edge, enclosing the seam allowance from the top tier.

7. Add closures where the waistband overlaps—heavy-duty hooks and eyes are great for this!

Cosplay Creative: Bambi Lashes Design

COSPLAYER: Bambi Lashes Design
COSTUME: Sarah from *Labyrinth*

Photo by Amie Photos

Instagram: @bambilashesdesign

My favorite reason for making my own crinolines is that it allows me to create the most dramatic and beautiful silhouettes, with so many possibilities. I love to experiment with underskirts, from the dramatic pannier silhouette I created for my cosplay of Sarah from *Labyrinth*, to the nipped-in fishtail silhouette for Mipha from *Breath of the Wild*. It's all about the hoops!

I took two completely different approaches with these gowns. For Sarah, I made a grand pannier in the style of eighteenth-century French court gowns. I used a historical approach and traditional materials for this process—hoop steel, linen fabric, and cotton cords. I opted to tweak the shape and details to match both my reference and my own taste. It's also important to make adjustments to suit your working space and materials!

For Mipha, I wanted to create a mermaid skirt with a dramatic silhouette. To achieve this, I constructed a crinoline that flared out from the knee using a hoop steel to keep the shape, attached to a spandex underskirt. Having this stretch base from the waist to the knee allowed me to achieve a super dramatic flair. It made it more comfortable to wear too—modifications for comfort can be just as important as those for aesthetics.

As you can see, there's so much room to explore and get creative when it comes to crinolines. Traditional shapes and methods are a perfect place to start, but don't be afraid to experiment as you grow your skills!

Other Undergarments

While the corset, hoop skirt, and petticoat are the most common undergarments for a ballgown cosplay, it's certainly not an exhaustive list! Especially for costumes pulling from specific historical periods, you may come across the following items: bumrolls, panniers, and pockets.

A heavy skirt without undergarments

A bumroll with a short petticoat for smoothing

The silhouette with undergarments

COSPLAYER: Cowbutt Crunchies

COSTUME: Marceline from *Adventure Time* (original design)

Photo by The World of Gwendana

BUMROLLS/PADS

Bumrolls are shaped fabric pillows attached to straps that tie around the waist and provide a bit of extra padding at the seat. While they are an essential piece of Elizabethan dress, they can be useful in other contexts:

* Under an elliptical hoop skirt to help keep it balanced backwards

* Under a more modern skirt that is especially heavy or dragging in the back

* As a travel pillow for the flight back home from a convention :)

PANNIERS

Panniers are similar to but different in construction from hoop skirts in that they are not fully circular. Instead, they are built as slightly squashed half-circles, designed to be worn, one on each side of the hip, to create an elliptical shape. The classic Marie Antoinette–style gown, with the wide skirts and flat front, is achieved by using panniers.

You do need a specific pattern to make panniers; however, many of the construction techniques and materials are the same as described in Hoop Skirts (page 48).

POCKETS

And no, we don't mean modern dress pockets! Undergarment pockets are based on the historical precursor to built-in pockets; they are designed to be worn under both petticoats and hoops and hang from the waist. While many cosplayers choose to simply build modern pockets into their skirts or default to a bag to get around a con, historical pockets can be a useful replacement and can be made to hold larger or heavier items that might detract from your skirt's silhouette.

If you're interested in using separate pockets as an undergarment, you need to create access from the outside of the garment by adding a slash opening in the fashion skirt, petticoats, and hoop skirt. If you can, use your construction seams to your advantage, and form the opening within the seam.

COSPLAYER:
Lunar Rose Costuming

COSTUME: Marie Antoinette
from *Marie Antoinette*

Photo by Alexandra Lee Studios

A huge part of cosplay design is proportion and silhouette. Fortunately for cosplayers, most common skirt silhouettes break down into a few basic shapes. While all shapes can create beautiful, elaborate gowns, there are some important construction differences to keep in mind.

THE SKIRT

COSPLAYER: Cowbutt Crunchies
COSTUME: Loki from *Thor* (original design)
Photo by Sorairo Days

Skirt Shapes

Bell/Cupcake

A-line/Circle

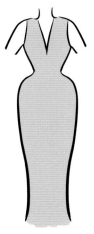

Sheath/Fitted

COSPLAYER: Ilabelle Cosplay

COSTUME: Belle from *Beauty and the Beast*

Photo by Mama Kat Photography

BELL/CUPCAKE

Bell-shaped or "cupcake" skirts have a large amount of swell right at the waistband. Whether you're making a skirt that is slightly full or a petticoat monster, the shape is created through gathering at the waist, with the bulk of the skirt falling evenly down the shape. This is commonly seen in traditional princess-type designs, Lolita-influenced styles, and many historical gowns.

COSPLAYER: Cowbutt Crunchies
COSTUME: Necromancer from Sakizo

Photo by DasGeminii

A-LINE/CIRCLE

A-line skirts have less bulk at the waistband than bell-shaped skirts and they add more fabric as they drop down. This creates a full, "swishy" skirt, which can be worn with or without a petticoat. Circle skirts are a beginner-friendly type of A-line that offer even more movement with a fitted waistline. They are good options for more modern styles, fancy versions of utilitarian designs, skirts with extreme trains, and cute, fluffy magical girls.

COSPLAYER: Coffee Cat Cosplay
COSTUME: Zelda from *The Legend of Zelda*

Photo by Solita D Photo

SHEATH/FITTED

While not as common in cosplay design as the other two shapes, these skirts can create a mature, elegant, or sexy silhouette. They generally have less volume throughout as they're designed to fit closely to the body. You are also more likely to see these as one-piece gowns, instead of a separate bodice and skirt, and they often require more patterning to fit. These can be great for runway versions of characters, certain historical periods, and villains.

COSPLAYER: Thranduart Cosplay
COSTUME: Lady Tremaine from *Cinderella*
Photo by Jason Laboy Photography

HYBRID SKIRT SHAPES

Understanding skirt construction allows you to alter and combine different aspects of each type of skirt to create truly custom styles. Building in excess and then gathering the waist of a circle skirt can create more volume on top to balance the bottom. Mermaid dresses, which are popular designs, are essentially sheath dresses with panels of a circle skirt patterned into the lower skirt. A bell-shaped skirt can become a magical girl skirt simply by shortening the length. Don't be afraid to experiment and combine techniques to bring some real wizardry to your cosplay!

COSPLAYER: Cowbutt Crunchies
COSTUME: Machine Queen (original design)
Photo by Alexandra lee Studios

Cosplay Creative: Thranduart Cosplay

Instagram: @thranduart.cosplay

Glinda is a costume near and dear to my heart. When I decided to create her, I was slightly nervous considering she would be my first ever true "ballgown." I also knew based on my sewing experience that the design was deceptively simple-looking and would probably present more than a few challenges ... and gosh if that didn't turn out to be true! My first obstacle was the shape of the skirt. This iconic silhouette was one I knew I wanted to get just right because the character is so important to me. I found a secondhand pattern online of a historical hoop structure called grand panniers that had a wide, almost square hip shape instead of a traditional round look you see in more modern gowns. To be sure, the skirt size was a near square proportion to my height (I'm 6'4" without heels). I extended the pattern both sideways and lengthwise, which meant adding an extra hoop at the bottom of the hoop skirt to increase the width by two feet.

I achieved the overall structure with steel hooping, ribbons tied together inside to hold the shape, and ruffled netting at the very bottom to help keep the skirt from dragging under the front edge when I walked forward. I also created my own "petticoat" using the same pattern. The petticoat is basically a slipcover to which I attached multiple layers of ruffles. This was important because I didn't want the rows of steel hooping to show under the skirt—I wanted the finished product to look soft and voluminous, as if it was completely made of tulle. The skirt itself is a single layer of taffeta, followed with 8 layers of lightweight tulle, and a final layer of a firm netting that I flatlined with the tulle. This final layer needed to be firm enough so it didn't drag down under the weight of the embellishments, but also airy enough to continue the illusion of floof. Ultimately, I am very pleased with the finished effect!

COSPLAYER: Thranduart Cosplay
COSTUME: Glinda from *The Wizard of Oz*
Photo by Solita D Photo

Patterning Your Skirt

Want to know a secret? Despite being one of the biggest parts of a gown's design and silhouette; despite being one of the most fun things on a ballgown to wear; despite the fact that they require yards and yards of petticoats and steel to keep them looking just right—the ballgown skirt is often the easiest part to make—at least in terms of basic construction! This is because most skirts can be boiled down to two basic shapes: squares and circles. The two most common elaborate cosplay skirt shapes are the basic bell shape and the circle skirt, both of which can be easily patterned from scratch using a few basic measurements and geometry.

Start with a design plan (see Creating a Project/Design Plan, page 17). You probably already have the measurements you need to draft a skirt pattern. Both the circle and the bell skirts require only two measurements: waist circumference and skirt length.

Waist circumference doesn't necessarily mean your natural waist. If you have a drop-waist design, or an empire waist, the "waist" of the skirt could rest on your hips or up around your ribs. As you work on your design plan (page 29), be sure to use the correct measurement for the desired "waist" location.

COSPLAYER: Raine Emery

COSTUME: Wedding Belle from *Beauty and the Beast* (original design)

Photo by Mapu Iosefa

Skirt length may not be as simple as the measurement from your waist to the floor because if your cosplay has bulky undergarments, there is length lost in the volume. If you have a hoop and petticoat ready, an easy way to check the length is to put on the undergarments and hold a cloth measuring tape at your waist and let it fall over the undergarments, making note on the tape where you want your final skirt hem. You can also use proportioned lengths or measurements from your plan. Otherwise, cut the skirt longer than you think you need.

If your design calls for a more fitted or narrow silhouette, like a sheath or column dress, you can still use the methods in this chapter—you just need to add less volume in your measurements! Elegant empire waist column gowns, for example, use the bell skirt method of construction, but with a "waist" circumference that is measured around the ribs and is half the finished skirt circumference of a true bell skirt (see bell or cupcake skirts, page 74). A smooth, fitted sheath dress is often a modified circle skirt, with a third or a quarter of a circle instead of a full or half-circle. Keep in mind, as you read this chapter, that choosing your skirt construction is as much about distribution of volume as it is about overall size of your gown. Do you want a more fitted upper part compared to the volume at the hem (circle skirt), or do you want a similar volume throughout the body of the skirt (bell skirt)?

Short Gowns

Want a short gown? No problem! To achieve that ultra-fluffy volume, follow the basic instructions for creating hoops or petticoats, but cut them to a shorter length. For hoop skirts, tighten the space between the upper bones so that they are arranged closer to your waist. For very short petticoats, build your petti with just two short tiers and focus on adding several layers to build out the volume. If you are trying to achieve a petticoat style that is wider than it is long, start lengthening the tiers as you build your layers outward, or the bottom of your skirt will visibly curve upward. This happens to all petticoats when the distance traveling outward becomes longer and longer with each pouf, but it is exaggerated with very short styles.

With any short skirt, consider wearing a pair of bloomers over your tights if modesty is a concern!

COSPLAYER: Cowbutt Crunchies
COSTUME: Amethyst from Sakizo
Photo by Shelley Cosplay & Photography

BELL OR CUPCAKE SKIRTS

Because these skirts start as rectangular pieces, the math to draft patterns for them is simple: All you need is the width and length of your rectangle!

• **WIDTH**   The width of your fabric rectangle corresponds to the skirt's bottom circumference and is key in determining how much volume will be packed into your final gown. The biggest mistake many people make is simply underestimating how much volume they want. There are tutorials that recommend a flat "waist times three" proportion, where the bottom circumference of the skirt is three times the measurement of your waist, but for a glorious, floor-length gown, that can look underwhelming. Instead, we recommend to first decide how large you'd like the circumference of the bottom of your gown to be. Anywhere between 120″ and 160″ is a great starting point for a grand cosplay gown! You reduce the circumference at the waist with gathers (or even small pleats or tucks).

If you already have your undergarments in hand, place your hoop skirt and/or petticoat on a dress form and then measure around the base to quickly determine your skirt circumference.

• **LENGTH**   To determine length, measure from your waist to the desired bottom edge of your gown while wearing your undergarments, allowing the measuring tape to drape over the petticoats. Write down this number as the skirt length on the Rectangle Skirt Planner (page 80).

• **PUTTING IT ALL TOGETHER**   Whenever possible, choose extra-wide 54″ or 60″ fabrics that are greater than your length measurement. If your measured length is less than that total fabric width, you can simply gather up a single long rectangle of fabric in the length calculated and sew a skirt from that! However, if your skirt length is greater than your fabric width, you'll need to rotate your pattern and combine several rectangular pieces to create a single, larger rectangle with the correct width and length.

Refer to the Rectangle Skirt Planner to calculate your final fabric measurement and account for seam allowances when you need to piece a rectangle. Add 1¼″ to each side of every rectangle for seam allowances.

Tip

It's important to remember that for the kind of fantastically huge skirts that cosplay gowns often call for, bell skirts are very dependent on their undergarments to achieve a silhouette of any size. For more standard garments, and more narrow gowns, adding pleats, tucks, and gathers to the waistband can add some pouf to the silhouette, but for a cosplay gown where you would like to achieve a 150″ skirt, be sure to add a large enough hoop or petticoat so that your undergarments also measure 150″.

Because the undergarments affect the finished size of a bell skirt so much, the finished circumference of your overall silhouette—how big around the skirt appears—is related to but not quite the same thing as the overall volume, or fullness, of the skirt itself. A bell skirt that is drafted to the exact finished circumference of your undergarments will be smooth and fitted at the bottom. If your design has a draped appearance, or you like the look of additional folds and swish, your drafted skirt measurement should be larger than the intended final circumference, and the excess fabric becomes additional volume without changing the overall finished circumference.

If you would like more swish and volume, add several inches to your intended final circumference and use that number going forward. Be sure to make note of the extra volume in your skirt planner.

Rectangle Skirt Planner

Skirt circumference (sc): _____

Skirt length (sl): _____

For a single rectangle:

Pattern width: sc + 1″ = _____

Pattern length: sl + 1¼″ = _____

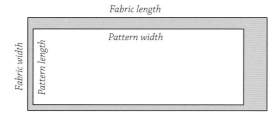

Fabric length

Pattern width

Fabric width

Pattern length

For more than one rectangle:

To determine the pattern width, divide the skirt circumference by the fabric width minus 1″. Round up to a whole number to find the number of rectangles needed. Divide the skirt circumference by the number of rectangles to find the pattern width.

For example, the skirt circumference is 160″. Subtract 1″ from the fabric width (60″ – 1″ = 59″). Divide 160″ by 59″ to equal 2.71; round up to 3. Divide 160″ by 3 to equal about 53½″.

Pattern width:

sc / fabric width – 1″ = # of rectangles (round up to whole number) = _____

sc / # of rectangles = _____

Pattern length: sl + 1¼″ = _____

Fabric length

Pattern length

Pattern width

Fabric width

CIRCLE SKIRTS

While some "circle skirt calculators" claim to eliminate the math behind drafting your own circle skirt, they are not ideal for cosplay purposes or for very large gowns.

To draft a circle skirt pattern, use the following formula: Circumference = 2 × pi (3.14) × master radius. Keep in mind that cutting a circle skirt involves calculating *two* circles—the inner circle, which becomes your waist opening, and the outer circle, which will be the skirt hem. *The biggest patternmaking mistake with a circle skirt is not accounting for your waist.*

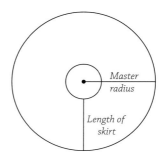

Master radius

Length of skirt

The *master radius* corresponds to the full radius of the circle you will cut from your fabric. Determine your master radius using the following steps:

1. First, calculate your *waist radius* by dividing your waist measurement by 6.28 (or 2 × pi) and then subtract ½″ from this measurement for the waistband seam allowance.

2. To calculate your *master radius*, add the desired skirt length + hem allowance to your waist radius from Step 1. We usually add 1½″ for hem allowance.

COSPLAYER: C0c0cosplays
COSTUME: Thumbelina from *Thumbelina*
Photo by Dinah Lee Bowles

MARKING AND CUTTING

1. Spread out your fabric in a single layer and mark the center point. This point is the very center of your imagined circles—so one full master radius length away from the fabric edges.

2. Use a long yardstick or measuring tape to mark both waist radius and master radius—almost like a giant compass drawing tool. To do this, mark the distance from the center point by carefully rotating the measuring tool and marking every inch or two. Connect the markings to draw each circle.

3. Unless you are using particularly wide fabric or cutting a shorter skirt, your circle will likely not fit onto a single piece of fabric. In this case, you need to split the skirt into 2 or more pieces, and then combine them back into the full circle shape.

- If your master radius is shorter than the width of the fabric, cut 2 half-circles, as shown. Just be sure to add a ½″ seam allowance for the new side seams.

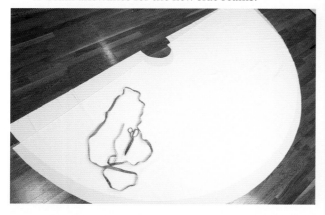

- If your master radius is longer than the width of the fabric, you need to cut the circle into several panels, or *gores*, laid out at an angle on the fabric. This requires more math and careful measuring, but the simplest way to think about this is to imagine the skirt as a pie that needs to be cut into several pieces.

1. Use your master radius to calculate the skirt's circumference. The curved edges of all of your panels will add up to that total.

2. Mark the fullest panels you can fit onto your fabric—remember to add a ½″ seam allowance for the side seams.

3. Measure the curved bottom edge of the panel and use that to calculate how many panels you need to create a whole circle.

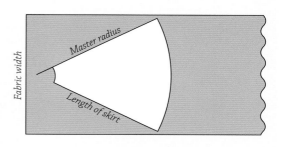

Tip

Don't be afraid to narrow the panel in order to place panels closer together in order to save on fabric. Alternatively, consider cutting the skirt front or back panel using a different measurement from the others and then using it as an opportunity for a fun feature panel, with its own contrasting fabric or decorations! Making mistakes into magic is a special part of cosplay.

4. Multiply the length of the panels by the number of panels to determine the amount of yardage needed.

An Important Cutting Note

While bell-shaped skirts are cut as rectangles, and therefore follow the grain of the fabric, portions of circle skirts are on the grain, while some portions are on the bias, which stretches. Sometimes the weight of the garment itself on the bias can stretch out the fabric permanently and cause wrinkling. So, after cutting your circle skirt, it is extremely important to hang your pieces up where they can relax and stretch before sewing anything together. Hang pieces overnight to allow them to totally relax—you may need to trim them a bit if they significantly stretch. To help the panels fully stretch, add sewing clips or clothespins for extra weight.

Skirt Construction

We always approach skirt assembly with an eye for what will produce the easiest, cleanest cosplay. For example, the lining should be attached after any embellishments in order to avoid unsightly stitching through the lining layer. Similarly, adding a waistband early helps you confidently see where the skirt will sit on your body, and thus where the hem and embellishments belong. However, don't be afraid to mix up the order of operations if your skirt includes a special feature that throws a wrench into the usual steps. For example, if your skirt includes swags or bustles, wait to attach the waistband until the swags are sewn into place. Your cosplay is uniquely yours. *Skirt construction, like all cosplay, should be thought through, step-by-step, before sewing a stitch.* However, for most skirts, we typically follow these steps:

1. Sew the vertical, joining seams (center back, side seams, and/or panel seams) to form one large tube of fabric for a bell skirt or one large circle or A-line shape with a waist opening for a circle skirt. Leave 3″–4″ unsewn at the waist edge of the backmost seam to give your skirt extra room to slide over your hips or shoulders. Press all seams. If you want pockets, now is the time to sew them into the side seams.

Tip

If your interior seams will be visible because of the skirt design, serge the seams or use a flat-felled seam for neatness (page 62).

COSPLAYER:
Cowbutt Crunchies

COSTUME: Princess Kenny from *South Park* (original design)

Photo by Amie Photos

2. Temporarily secure the waist:

● For a circle skirt, run a basting stitch ⅝″ from the waist edge to keep it from stretching or deforming while you work on the rest of the skirt.

● For a bell skirt, gather the waist (see Gathering Methods, page 64) and then baste the fabric into place so it is stable.

For either skirt type, you can also baste a narrow ¼″ piece of grosgrain ribbon along the waist edge for extra stability while working.

3. If you have multiple skirt layers arranged on top of each other, or will be incorporating swags, pickups, or peplums into the waistline, do so now. Create each additional piece separately and try them all on at once to verify placement before pinning them together at the waistline. Once you're happy with the fit and placement, baste together the layers.

4. Make and apply the waistband (see Make the Waistband, page 67) *unless you are planning on lining your skirt*. Generally, we only use a true lining on smaller, lighter-weight gowns or if stitching inside the skirt will be visible. If your skirt is exceptionally large or heavy, you may want to consider cleanly hemming and finishing your seams instead. If you plan on lining the skirt instead of hemming, install your waistband after Step 7.

5. Using the temporary waist, try on the skirt with your undergarments to check the length. Pin and hem the bottom edge of the skirt.

6. Add embellishments, such as lace, embroidery, and appliqué. Or, other elements like snaps, hidden straps, and magnetic catches for non-sewn elements like armor, magic gems, LED panels, and other materials.

7. Finish your skirt by installing a lining if desired. The lining should match the skirt shape and should be assembled following the instructions in Step 1. Sew the lining to the bottom edge of the skirt, right sides together. Turn so the wrong sides are together and press. Align and pin the waistline edges together and follow the instructions for adding a waistband in Step 4.

8. Add closures. You have a few options.

For heavier fabrics Install a zipper in the entire back opening or attach heavy-duty hooks and eyes to the waistband and smaller ones on the rest of the back opening.

For very light or sheer skirts Add a narrower waistband in a matching fabric that will be visible or even create an elastic waist.

Hemming Tips

Hemming circle skirts is something even veteran cosplayers struggle with!

• For a narrow double-fold hem, use a lot of pins and press the hem before you start sewing.

• Depending on your fabric, you can do a rolled hem, but you need a specialty presser foot.

• You can also use bias binding to create a faced edge, and it produces a fun finish!

• Because hemming creates a long horizontal line at the bottom of the skirt, be sure to finish the hem before applying any lace, appliqué, or other trim that lies on top of this edge.

• Adding horsehair braid to a hem adds body to a skirt (see How to Install Horsehair Braid, page 86).

• Take it slow!

How to Add Horsehair Braid to a Hem

Horsehair braid (which in modern times is made of polyester) is like a secret ingredient, adding oomph and body to your skirt's hem. It comes in a few basic colors and many different widths. While the narrower widths are fantastic for adding body to ruffles, sleeves, or peplums, when it comes to ballgowns and other formal cosplay skirts, it's best to use wider widths, between 3″ and 6″ depending on the weight of your fabric. Heavier, more full-bodied fabrics such as satin benefit from thicker braid.

HOW TO INSTALL HORSEHAIR BRAID

The skirt before installing horsehair braid

The skirt after installing horsehair braid

1. Allow ½″ for hem allowance when drafting a pattern.

2. Try on your skirt to determine the finished hem length; mark the location with pins.

3. Cut a length of horsehair braid the length of your skirt circumference plus ½″. Some horsehair braid has an extra gathering string woven into one edge. If your horsehair has this string, orient it toward the waistband when you pin the braid to the skirt.

4. Pin the horsehair braid on the right side of the fabric. Be careful not to stretch it as you pin it around the skirt. The two bound ends can overlap each other slightly.

Tip
The ends of horsehair braid can be messy and itchy, so use a piece of bias tape or scrap skirt fabric to bind them.

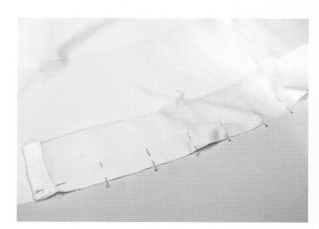

5. Sew through both the skirt and the horsehair braid, ¼″ in from the edge of the braid and ¼″ from the fabric edge. Remove all pins.

6. Use an iron on low to medium heat to press the braid away from the skirt. Allow the skirt hem allowance to fold under completely; don't press a fold into the braid where the seam was sewn.

7. Turn the horsehair braid to the inside of the skirt. Press.

8. Turn the skirt inside out and lay it flat. If your horsehair braid has the gathering thread, gently pull on it to gather the excess braid until it lies smoothly against the skirt. If your braid doesn't have a gathering thread, use pins to evenly distribute any extra fullness.

9. Make sure the braid hasn't been pulled, twisted, or rippled, and then carefully pin the upper, loose edge of the braid to keep it in place. Topstitch the top edge of the braid in place.

10. Turn the skirt right side out and marvel at the difference horsehair makes!

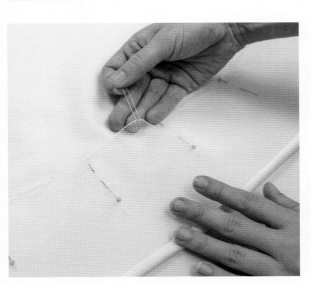

Appendages and Attachments

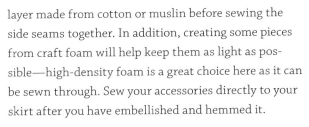

Sometimes cosplay designs take an already fabulous ballgown design out of this world with the addition of tails, massive embellishments, armor, or other decidedly un-ballgown-like additions. While you should start thinking about the way these will be incorporated early in your design plan, you absolutely should nail down the specifics prior to completing your skirt, to avoid having to take it apart or totally start over.

* *Armor panels* around the hips, or *jewels* surrounding the bottom edge, are heavy and require fabric with some structure to prevent pulling. To strengthen a more delicate skirt, interline each piece with a strength

layer made from cotton or muslin before sewing the side seams together. In addition, creating some pieces from craft foam will help keep them as light as possible—high-density foam is a great choice here as it can be sewn through. Sew your accessories directly to your skirt after you have embellished and hemmed it.

* A *large appendage like a dragon tail or branches* almost always needs to be mounted to your body using a harness or separate structural undergarment. This prevents the weight from resting completely on your garment's structures, which usually aren't designed for so much additional weight. When planning your garment, do additional research based on the size, shape, and any movement you wish to incorporate, so you can have a good plan for how the main garment and the appendage will work together. It's also a good idea to build your appendage first, so you can continue to adjust your skirts during patterning and fitting in case of unexpected issues!

* If the appendage is something that *appears behind you* and if there is a center back seam, you may be able to simply leave it partially open to fit around the piece. Alternatively, you can cut a hole to fit and finish with a facing, depending on positioning of the skirt and the prop.

* *Huge, magical-girl–style bows* should be made first and then attached to the skirt.

Often, attaching the bow directly to the skirt will cause it to pull or buckle. Instead, consider using structured undergarments, like a hoop skirt, as the main support. High-powered magnets can be sewn into the base of the bow with the matching magnet in a tiny pocket sewn to the hoop skirt. Heavy-duty snaps can also work, though you would need to leave a small opening in the skirt for them to snap through.

COSPLAYER: Cowbutt Crunchies
COSTUME: Machine Queen (original design)
Photo by Sorairo Days

COSPLAYER:
Cowbutt Crunchies

COSTUME: Helgasercle
from *Tree of Savior*

Photo by Sorairo Days

Once the skirt is complete, it's time to create the bodice! Depending on your design plan and measurements, this could be as simple as re-creating a three-piece pattern for a sleeveless top, or it could involve a boned, altered-neckline bodice with princess seams and customized sleeves. Bodices require smaller pieces than skirts, but due to their fit and variation, they require a good deal of tailoring and planning ahead.

THE BODICE

COSPLAYER: Cowbutt Crunchies

COSTUME: Deku Princess from *The Legend of Zelda* (original design)

Photo by David Sohno

Planning Your Bodice

There are several things to consider when planning your bodice.

* Is your costume historically influenced? Is your corset specific to the historical period? If so, your bodice should reflect the same time-period, so it fits over the corset.

* How will the bodice open? Will openings be obvious or hidden? Do you even need an opening? We usually use a center back opening, but your bodice might need to be different.

* What type of neckline are you planning? Is it a strapless or a high collared bodice? Are there straps? Are there sleeves? What shape are the sleeves?

* How structured is your fabric and design? Will you drape the bodice with bias-cut panels, or is it a structured, fitted top? Is it a combination bodice with a structured base and fabric draped around it? Check your sources carefully; this can be tricky to determine. Generally, if the bodice looks like it is fitted to the character's body, you should anticipate building a structured lining and then adding additional fabric drapery.

COSPLAYER: Knit Freak Cosplay
COSTUME: Snow White from Sakizo
Photo by Adoylible

STARTING WITH A PATTERN

Much like corsets, bodices deal with complex curves and variated sizing. However, unlike corsets, they have the added complication of sleeves, shoulder straps, and collars. Starting with a pattern—whether a commercial pattern, a draped sloper, or a self-drafted block—is essential. Unless you are comfortable with drafting and fitting, it is a good idea to start with a commercial pattern, especially if you are working with a complex design.

As you search for a commercial pattern in the costume or formal section of the pattern catalogs (or online), don't fret about finding an exact match. Altering a pattern to fit your needs is a tried-and-true cosplay tradition: A pattern for a sundress can be cut at the waist to turn it into a bodice. A pattern with a high-necked collar can be reshaped into an off-the-shoulder look. And sleeves can be altered to be longer, shorter, fuller, or slimmer. However, there are a few important things to look for in a pattern.

* Seamlines that match your design. While a dress with a raglan sleeve can be lovely, if your design calls for traditional sleeves, altering the pattern for a regular armhole is difficult. Similarly, if you want a bodice with princess seams, which are flattering on a variety of body types, look for a bodice pattern that includes them to begin with.

* If your design has sleeves, purchase a pattern that includes at least a basic sleeve. Sleeve alterations can be done easily with paper and a ruler, but if you're already buying a pattern, it's much easier to alter an existing sleeve pattern than to start from nothing.

* Do patterns usually fit you without modifications or will you need to make alterations? If you are between sizes, purchase the larger size—it's easier to take a garment in than to let it out.

* If you anticipate needing to make alterations, buy a simpler pattern. Pattern companies produce patterns for tops with lots of interesting construction and unusual sewing details, but all the additional pieces make alterations difficult. A pattern with two front pieces, one or two back pieces, and a sleeve is all you need (sometimes a collar is helpful).

* Historical compatibility with your corset, if applicable. A 1908 bodice will not fit over eighteenth-century stays without alterations.

COSPLAYER: Ivorivet

COSTUME: Pincushion
(original design)

Photo by Implode

MOCKING UP YOUR TEST BODICE

We strongly recommend making a test bodice out of muslin or cheap cotton. Not only will you be able fix fit issues, but you can begin altering the neckline, the seamlines, or anything else your heart desires! While flat patternmaking works well for skirts and other garments, it is easier to modify a bodice pattern while you—or your dress form—are wearing it.

Mocking Up for Fit

Use a cheap, light fabric for your mock-up, such as muslin, fabric from your stash, cheap cottons, or even cheap thrift store sheets! Try to use light-colored fabric so it's easier to see any design lines or fitting marks you make.

1. Cut and baste the bodice pieces together per the pattern instructions, ignoring any permanent closures, like zippers. If the pattern has sleeves, you only need to cut out and attach one. Install a temporary closure like a basted zipper, or hook and eye tape or have a friend pin and unpin the bodice closed for you. Ignore all finishing instructions, like hems, linings, and facings.

2. Put on your undergarments that will affect the fit of the bodice, including any corsets, bras, body shapers, and, depending on where your waist is and how long your bodice is, your hoop skirt and skirts. Turn your mock-up inside out so that the seams are exposed and then put it on over your undergarments.

3. Use a fabric marker or chalk to mark your possible alterations. Consider the following fit questions.

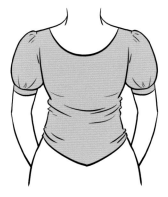

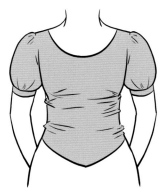

- *Check the waistline.* If the bodice is folding or bunching where it hits your skirts, then it is too long. Mark directly on the mock-up where the waist should end on the bodice. Add seam allowances for finishing the bottom edge and then cut off the extra length.

- *Check the size.* Is it too large? Too small? Bodies are rarely the same size all the way through so your bodice may be too large in some areas and too small in others.

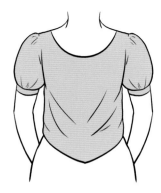

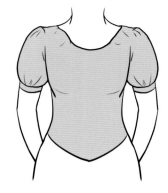

Too small: A good way to tell if the garment is too small, even if it's not uncomfortable, is if it pulls from other areas of the bodice. You will see diagonal wrinkles developing. If you think an area is too small, use a seam ripper and carefully open a small amount of the nearest seam until the wrinkles ease out. Take note of how wide that opening is at the fabric's edge—you'll need to add that amount to the pattern when you recut it. Remember that this amount needs to be split between the two joined pattern pieces, so when you cut out your new pieces, divide the amount you want to add to the bodice in half and extend the edges of each piece by that amount.

When you change a seamline by adding fabric, you'll want to draw a new cutting line. Place a dot at the point where you started seam ripping and draw a smooth line. If you need to add more fabric to establish a wider cutting line, attach a fabric scrap (or piece of paper) to indicate the added width for the new pattern piece. We often also write directly on the mock-up using a marker or pen, to indicate how much we're adding.

Too large: If your garment is too large, it lifts away from your body and is often concentrated in loose folds at the seams. Carefully pinch and pin some of the excess fabric out at the seams. Don't pin all the excess out of just one seam, because that often causes the bodice to pull or buckle elsewhere. For a too-large waist, for example, try pinching some fabric out of the side seam, some from the front-side seam, and some from the back. And remember to always mirror any pinning on the other side! Once you're happy with the fit, take the bodice off and mark a line along the pins, restitch, and try the bodice on again.

Check the shoulders and the neck. For non-strapless bodices, check that the seams fit smoothly over your shoulders. They might need to be pinned in or let out like the vertical seams.

Check the sleeve. Is it comfortable? Too tight? Too loose? Sleeve alterations for style are covered in the next section, but they can be adjusted for fit now. If you need to adjust the sleeve where it joins the bodice, you *also* need to alter the armhole itself. If you are inexperienced with flat-patternmaking from

scratch, or just find sleeve math intimidating, take advantage of your pattern's multiple sizes to trace a new sleeve mock-up in the next size up or down, as needed. Then use the matching size line on the bodice pattern to re-trace *only* the armhole on your bodice mock-up. If the rest of the bodice fits, you don't need to make any other size changes.

- If this makes the armhole bigger, simply cut the fabric away along the traced line.

- If this makes your armhole smaller, you probably need to baste or pin scrap fabric under the existing armhole so you can trace the new cutting line. Sometimes it's easier to recut the bodice pieces entirely with the resized armhole.

Sometimes you need a lot of fit alterations and sometimes you're lucky and the modifications are minimal. For substantial fit changes, it's worth taking the mock-up off, seam-ripping it apart, and drafting a new mock-up based on the alterations. With the second mock-up, redraw the pattern edges to reflect shrinkage in places where you sewed tighter stitch lines and increases in places where you split seams. Remember to retain your seam allowances! Cut the new pieces and baste them together. Try the test bodice on again to verify that fit problems are fixed.

If you're happy with that mock-up, you're ready to move on to style alterations.

Mocking up for Style

With your newly-fitted mock-up bodice, it's time to consider style and design alterations. Keep your design plan nearby so you can determine how you need to alter the test bodice to best match your character reference. Consult the plan and determine where it differs from the mock-up. It's really a lot of fun to modify the mock-up and make it match your design plan!

1. Put the mock-up bodice on with the necessary undergarments. An easy way to visualize your finished design is to sketch any potential alterations directly onto your bodice mock-up.

2. Use a marker, pen, or chalk to draw where you want your new hems, edges, seams, and other details to be (see Design Modifications, page 96). Don't like what you drew? Try again in a darker color! Don't worry about including seam allowances for now—it's easier to picture the final garment with its finished edges. Seam allowances can always be added back in later.

3. Once all the desired modifications are marked, remove the bodice and rip open the seams or cut any new hemlines.

4. Trace the design lines from the final modifications onto heavy paper or poster board, adding any missing seam allowances to your altered hemlines. Transferring the pattern onto new paper allows you to

● smooth out any awkward lines resulting from marking it while wearing it,

● make sure you've added back consistent seam allowances everywhere they're needed,

● transfer important guides or notches from the original pattern to the new customized pattern, and

● most importantly, keep all your work for future projects! A custom-fitted pattern can be used for many upcoming cosplays, without the need to re-fit and re-tailor!

NECKLINE   Draw a new neckline to make it wider or lower. Or draw design lines for an incredibly deep V or a sweetheart neckline. Simply cut on the design lines and try the test bodice back on and see how you like the new neckline!

Tip

Sometimes we experiment by drawing two different neckline options—one on the left side and one on the right side—using the center front as the split line. If you like one of the necklines, mirror the design lines on the other side.

COLLAR   If the collar is a basic style, try to find a similar pattern that is a close match or one that you can easily modify. Slashing and spreading a pattern (page 99) can be used to modify existing collar patterns into all kinds of shapes. However, for especially large or elaborate collars that require stiff interfacing to hold their shape, sketch the shape you want on poster board or foam. Cut it out and hold it up to the test bodice. Recut the test collar until you have the size and scale you want. Use the poster board or foam as a pattern when you are making the bodice from fashion fabric.

CLOSURE   While a center back zipper closing is common and often perfect for cosplay, it might not always work for your design. Generally, you can install a zipper in any seam, including the side seam, provided it crosses the narrowest part of your waist. Or forgo a zipper completely and use buttons, hooks and eyes, or lacing.

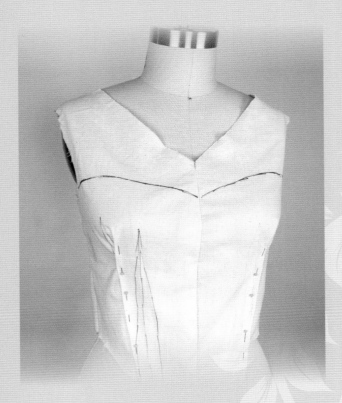

STRAPLESS Stand in front of a mirror and draw a line across the top of the bodice, following a straight or sweetheart shape. Use the bottom of the armhole as a guide as you mark around your torso. You might find it helpful to have a friend mark around your back.

WAIST SHAPE Do you want a straight edge or a deep V at the bottom of your bodice? You can mark anywhere you'd like to remove fabric, or pin scrap fabric to expand the mock-up to better visualize the shape.

SLEEVE LENGTH Do the sleeves need to be longer or shorter? To shorten, just draw a line around the sleeve mock-up where you want a hem or a cuff. To lengthen, it's easier to measure the distance from the bottom of the sleeve to where you'd like the new edge to be—make note of the measurement and add that amount to the bottom of the sleeve pattern. Other, more intense sleeve modifications require a bit more patterning (see Customizing Sleeves on the next page).

Customizing Sleeves

Whether your design calls for short, round puffs or long, dragging bells, sleeves have a huge impact on your overall costume design. Learning to understand how mass in sleeves works and how to alter a sleeve pattern to achieve a custom look is a valuable cosplay skill that translates not just across ballgowns, but into the wider cosplay world. All of the following modifications can be made using the slash-and-spread method.

COSPLAYER: Dresses and Capes
COSTUME: Belle from *Beauty and the Beast*
Photo by Itsjustnovice

The Slash and Spread Pattern-Alteration Method

Many common alterations found in a ballgown design use the same slash and spread technique.

1. Try on your bodice mock-up and decide if you want to increase volume anywhere on your sleeve. This can be at your shoulders, your wrists, or in the case of princess-style puff sleeves, the entire sleeve. Hold a flexible measuring tape in a loose circle around the area to estimate how large you want that portion of the sleeve to become.

2. Once you know the desired circumference for your sleeve, measure the mock-up pattern at that same location. Subtract the mock-up's circumference from your desired circumference to find the difference and how much you need to add.

3. Copy your pattern or mock-up sleeve onto a large piece of paper or posterboard. Cut on the outer edges.

4. Use a large ruler to draw a line perpendicular to the bottom of sleeve. Measure and mark a vertical line 1˝ from where the arm seamline meets the bottom edge. Continue to mark lines 1˝ apart between the top and bottom of the sleeve, with the last line at least 1˝ from the opposite edge of the pattern. The sleeve should now be split into several even sections.

5. Depending on how much volume you are adding and where you are adding it, cut on the lines almost, but not completely through, starting at the edge with the increase (see Customizing Sleeves, page 98). There should be a tiny amount of paper connecting the pattern pieces. This is the *slash* step.

6. Place the pattern on an additional piece of poster board or paper. Using masking tape, secure one outside edge of the pattern so it doesn't shift. Divide the desired amount of volume you want to add from Step 2 between the number of lines you drew. This is the *spread* step.

For example, if you want to add 5˝ of puff to your sleeve and you drew 5 slash lines, spread the slash lines 1˝ apart. Secure with masking tape. Do this for each section of the sleeve. This is the spread. You can now trace around the modified pattern and your new sleeve will include all the new volume.

Adding Volume at the Shoulder

Slash from the top of the sleeve to the bottom edge, leaving the pattern connected at the bottom. Spread the sections and trace a new pattern. Once you've sewn this new sleeve, gather the extra fabric in the sleeve cap so that it still fits in the armhole. This gathering produces the pouf.

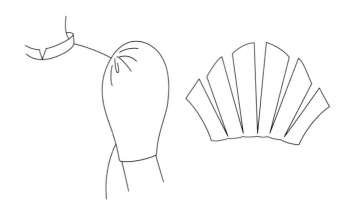

Adding Volume at the Bottom Edge

Slash from the bottom to the top of the sleeve, leaving the pattern connected at the top of the sleeve. This produces large, open bell sleeves if you don't gather the lower edge, or it produces poufed bishop-style sleeves by gathering the lower edge back to a smaller measurement.

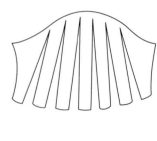

Princess-Style Puff Sleeves

1. First determine the desired sleeve length, as this short style tends to stop at the upper arm. If shortening the sleeve, be sure to allow for seam allowances or hems.

2. To add volume at both the top and bottom of the sleeve, cut the marked sections and separate them completely. Spread the strips in equal amounts throughout. Adding an especially large pouf can cause sleeves to shorten—to counteract this, we suggest adding 2″ along the pattern bottom edge. When constructing the sleeve, gather extra fabric at both the top and bottom.

Bell Sleeves

1. For sleeves that are fitted and then flare dramatically around the forearm, first decide where the flare should begin. Draw a line across the pattern to bisect the sleeve into a top and bottom portion. Cut along this line to split your mock-up or pattern.

2. There are two options to make the pattern for the bottom portion of the sleeve:

For more modest bells or a moderate flare: Draft a bell shape by marking lines at 1″ intervals from bottom to top edge. Slash the pattern from the bottom, leaving a small amount connected at the top. Spread the sections to add volume to the bottom edge. Trace to create a new lower-sleeve pattern. Make sure to add a ½″ seam allowance to the edges where the two sleeve pieces meet.

For extra-large, dramatic flares: Draft and cut a full circle to fit your arm, using the instructions in Circle Skirts (page 80). Measure your arm circumference at the bisect line and substitute this number in the instructions for the waist circumference. Measure your desired sleeve length from the bisect line and subtract this number in the instructions for the skirt length. Remember to add a ½″ seam allowance to the lower edge of the upper portion of the sleeve and to the inner circle edge of the sleeve lower portion so you can sew the pieces together without losing length.

3. Cut and sew the sleeve upper and lower portions together at the bisect line.

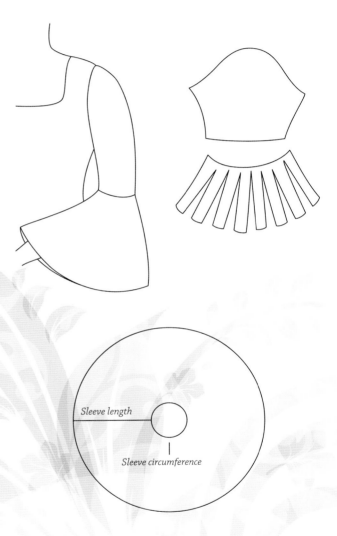

Sleeve length

Sleeve circumference

COSPLAYER: Cowbutt Crunchies

COSTUME: Ivysaur from *Pokémon* (original design)

Photo by Kameraninja

Constructing Your Bodice

Once you have the fit and design of your bodice pattern set, the hardest part is over! Depending on your fabric, construction may be as simple as cutting your pieces from fashion and lining fabrics, and putting the whole thing together the same way you did for the mock-ups. However, there are some construction details to keep in mind.

PREPARING AND CUTTING THE FABRICS

Most non-corseted bodices are constructed from two layers: a front-facing fashion layer and an interior lining layer that rests against the skin. However, depending on your choice of fabric, your fashion layer may require an extra step: an interlining.

Interlining or Flatlining

Hold one of your fashion fabric pieces between your hands. Does it feel thin or tend to buckle? Flatlining is a technique that increases the fashion layer's body and prevents wrinkling by reinforcing a lightweight fabric with a sturdier interlining, such as a medium-weight, inexpensive cotton. It is much like adding a strength layer of fabric to a corset. Heavier fabrics like upholstery weights or duchess satins often have enough body that they can simply be cut as is, without the need for flatlining. Lighter, thinner fabrics like dupioni, thin satin, or taffeta can benefit from an interlining layer, which requires you to cut another full set of pattern pieces from a third fabric, different from your fashion fabric and lining.

1. Match and stack each piece of interlining together with the corresponding fashion piece, placing wrong sides together so the fashion layer's right side is still visible. If your fashion fabric is slippery, spray baste with quilting spray before aligning pieces.

2. Baste the layers for each piece around all the edges with a very narrow seam allowance, locking the fashion fabric to the interlining.

Tip

If you don't want to flatline the fashion fabric, you can interface the pieces, but often that can add too much rigidity. Fusible interfacing, especially, can walk the line between too much support and unneeded stiffness, and too little support. However, if you plan on adding particularly heavy or dense embellishment in one area of your bodice, such as thick embroidery or sew-on jewels, interfacing the back of that area can help support the weight and keep your fabric from puckering or pulling.

Lining

Lining a bodice is almost always a good idea. Not only does it make for a more comfortable garment, but it hides raw edges, and prevents wear and tear to any seams, boning, and interior stitching from embellishments.

We usually install the lining after everything else—after adding boning, embellishments, and installing a zipper. The exception is if the bodice closure is buttons; in this case the buttonholes should be constructed through both the fashion and lining layers. You can also use the lining to secure embellishments. For example, by inserting the edge of a length of lace between the bodice and lining, and stitching it in along the seam, you have a lovely lace edging emerging from the edge flawlessly.

WEARING A CORSET UNDER A BODICE

If you are wearing a corset under the bodice, a well-fitted, lined bodice often doesn't need additional support besides basic interlining. If the corset is highly structural, it should provide smooth lines so the bodice fits over it smoothly. If you find occasional wrinkles or small areas of buckling in the bodice, you can add a few small pieces of boning to the bodice (see Boned Bodices, page 47) to fix the issues, but largely your bodice should be ready to wear.

If you're not wearing a corset under the bodice, consider adding corset boning in a few limited areas to add some structure to the bodice. This prevents folding and buckling, especially around the bust area, which can be difficult to manage—on strapless bodices especially! See Installing Boning (page 40).

HOW TO MAKE A CORSETED BODICE

Sometimes your cosplay might be better suited to a corseted bodice. Corseted bodices fit snugly and are great vehicles for heavy embellishment as they have more structural integrity than a regular bodice. However, when and how to embellish these bodices requires forethought. Anything from decorative panels to lace edging to weighty structural elements can be added, but you need to plan when and how to add both the boning and the embellishments. Our Necromancer bodice is a good example of a corseted bodice with lots of special elements. Adding embellishments at the right time in the construction process saves time and effort.

Every cosplay is unique, but in general we follow these steps:

1. Begin to construct your corseted bodice per your corset pattern's instructions, following guidelines for a typical corset undergarment in Corset Construction (page 37). This includes basic fabric assembly and sewing the boning channels. This stage is when different-colored panels or false closures would be installed.

2. Apply any embellishments that do not cross the boning channels. Install any built-in elements like snaps or magnets for supporting armor or other embellishments.

3. Continue with installing the boning and complete your corset, including finishing any raw edges and installing the closure.

4. Hand sew or glue any embellishments that are placed across the boning channels.

Tip

Remember: Once the boning is fully installed, don't use your sewing machine to attach anything else. A machine needle hitting a steel bone risks damaging your machine, or worse, breaking off and flying at your face.

COSPLAYER: Cowbutt Crunchies
COSTUME: Necromancer by Sakizo
Photo by DasGeminii

COSPLAY CONSTRUCTION CHALLENGES

As with so many other garments, there is a way to build a beautiful, traditional ballgown bodice—and then there is the challenge of building a beautiful cosplay ballgown bodice. Cosplay designs can push the limits of how traditional construction works, and often what works under normal circumstances doesn't hold up to a long day having fun at a convention.

The Challenges

The beauty of cosplay sewing is that the challenges often lead to very cool and creative solutions. Nothing is better than taking a design that really only works in a fictional setting and making it into a real, wearable garment, but still maintaining the over-the-top aspect!

- **PUFF SLEEVES**   Sewing instructions for puff sleeves often suggest including elastic at the bottom edge, to help it stay gathered and snug on your arm. If the sleeve slides down your arm, it depuffs. In our experience, elastic can be finicky and often needs adjusting, and we have spent plenty of hours pushing sleeves back up after swinging a prop sword or climbing up on a photogenic rock. A better technique for keeping puffed, gathered shapes in place, whether princess sleeves, renaissance trunk hose, magical-girl bloomers, or any other puffed garment, is to secure your puffs to a smaller structure such as an inner sleeve, which prevents the sleeve from slipping.

Tip

Creating an Inner Sleeve

This tip works best using a modified commercial pattern, as discussed earlier in this chapter (page 98).

1. Cut two sets of sleeves from the fashion fabric. If your fashion fabric is heavy or bulky, cut the inner sleeve set from muslin or a matching cotton.

- Cut the set of outer, puffed sleeves using the customized pattern.

- Cut the set of inner sleeves using the original, unmodified commercial pattern. However, instead of cutting the full length of the sleeve, cut it so it ends where you want the modified sleeve to end on your arm, plus seam allowance.

2. Sew each modified puff sleeve, including the gathers you added to shape the sleeve. Set aside. Sew each inner sleeve.

3. Pin the inner sleeve and puff sleeve at the bottom opening with right sides together. Stitch with a ½˝ seam allowance (or whatever seam allowance you prefer).

4. Turn the inner sleeve inside the puff sleeve so wrong sides are together. Think of the inner sleeve as a lining for the puff sleeve.

5. Line up the top edges of each gathered puff sleeve and inner sleeve. Pin and baste them together with a ¼˝ seam allowance.

6. Treat each sleeve as one piece and install them into the bodice armholes.

COSPLAYER: Cowbutt Crunchies

COSTUME: The Forest Spirit from *Princess Mononoke* (original design)

Photo by Sam Saturn

BODICES WITH OPEN SECTIONS

Heart- or circle-shaped openings over the bust, open backs, or bodices that are made out of flowers are common in fantasy and anime. Mark smaller or odd-shaped cutouts during the mock-up stage, remembering to add a small seam allowance. When constructing the bodice, add interfacing to the wrong side before cutting the opening. Apply a matching facing to the opening.

For cosplayers who are concerned with modesty or for bodices that feature large cutouts or simply don't have enough solid areas in the design to form a bodice, consider swapping out part or all of your fabric with illusion mesh. This is a very fine, light tulle/net that often comes in a variety of skin tones. It's often used in bridal and dancing costumes to create bodice sections that are nearly invisible. However, avoid the heavier, stretch illusion fabric that is often sold under the same name and is often used in ice skating or athletic costumes.

Always use a double layer of mesh for any replaced areas for strength. Mesh layers are ideal for strapless gowns with embellishments climbing over the top of the bodice. This way you have a whole bodice, but the upper portion is made of illusion fabric.

The Challenges continued

ADDING LARGE APPENDAGES OR OTHER STRUCTURES

You need to consider how any large accessories will be designed into your bodice. Wings, for example, are incredibly popular in designs across all media and are the bane of many cosplayers due to the weight, difficulty in keeping them stable, and lack of any obvious attachment points in the costume design itself.

Not all wings are heavy, but all wings require some way to attach to your cosplay and many also need support. Lightweight fairy wings are often manufactured with a long loop of wire that tucks directly into the lacing of a corseted bodice. While this works for ultra-light wings, heavier ones usually require a shoulder harness and that needs a bit more engineering. One less visible solution is to wear the harness under your costume. With this trick, the cosplayer cuts a small, unnoticeable hole in the bodice at the point where the wing attaches to the harness, typically around a slot or a buckle. This prevents any unsightly straps from showing and gives the impression that the wings are springing out directly from the body.

This style of strapping can also work for other bulky items, like armor and other items made from foam. Alternatively, use a bit of scrap fabric to wrap any strapping that can't be hidden—turning it into a design feature or helping it blend into your fashion fabric.

The attachment point for Seraphim's wings (for full design, see pages 5 and 50).

Cosplay Creative: CocoaSugar Cosplay

Instagram: @cocoasugarcosplay

This cosplay of Anthy Himemiya as designed by the artist Dessi-Desu was my first time attempting a ball-gown with any sort of volume or structure. I knew I would need a petticoat to give the skirt body and that the bodice would require boning. I had created petticoats before and felt more confident in my skills for that part, but not so much when it came to the structured bodice. If I had any advice to impart to other cosplayers, it's not to be afraid to fail; even with a mock-up, my first try at the bodice was far from what I wanted.

The waist was too big, the cups too small, and there was absolutely no support in the bust. I made a couple different attempts before I was satisfied.

Honestly, trial and error is the best way to learn, and your seam ripper is your best friend! A dress form is also helpful when you need to make adjustments. The hardest issue to fix was the bust support problem. Though the look matched the design created by the artist, there just wasn't enough stability in the bust for my comfort level. In the end, I sacrificed an old bra to help give extra support and so I felt comfortable. I think it's easy to get caught up in "the right way" to create things (and there are definitely tried-and-true techniques for creating ballgowns that are important to learn!), but never forget that ultimately, you're making it for yourself. Don't be afraid to make tweaks to a costume in order to make it your own—for comfort and style.

COSPLAYER: CocoaSugar Cosplay

COSTUME: Anthy Himemiya from *Revolutionary Girl Utena* (original design)

Photo by Felix Dandy

With your bodice laced and your skirts pressed, you're ready to don your brand-new ballgown and waltz onto the convention floor, right? Well, maybe not! Wearing large, sometimes unwieldy gowns requires a few extra steps, not to mention the extra embellishments one might want to add as the crowning jewel of such an elaborate cosplay!

FINISHING TOUCHES

COSPLAYER: Cowbutt Crunchies

COSTUMES: Princess Celestia and Queen Chrysalis from *My Little Pony* (original designs)

Photo by Sara Lynn Photography

Embellishing

What's an elaborate gown without a little extra pizazz? While not always necessary, adding trims, lace, and other embellishments can help elevate a ballgown and add more eye-pleasing details. An important thing to keep in mind when planning and creating embellishments is that many times the materials and techniques overlap—you can use rhinestones to accent your lace, or use ribbon as your embroidery "thread," or create appliqué out of beaded pieces. Experiment and think outside the box!

COSPLAYER: CocoaSugar Cosplay

COSTUME: Anthy Himemiya from *Revolutionary Girl Utena* (original design)

Photo by Felix Dandy

Tip

Embellishing your ballgown doesn't always mean adding as much bling as possible! First consider what mood and style is appropriate for your character or for your gown. For example, a Victorian mechanic would probably choose a less flashy dress rather than one covered in rhinestones. Consult your reference and inspiration photos before getting started.

TYPES OF EMBELLISHMENTS

Appliqué

Appliqué is the application of a secondary solid piece of material—whether simply fabric, fused vinyl, lace, a beaded overlay—onto your garment. It's a great, high-impact way to add embellishment and can create anything from solid, shaped trim along a skirt or cape to detailed gold flourishes on a stomacher or tabard. There are so many types of appliqués with different attachment methods.

Handmade appliqués can be made of almost any fabric and double-sided fusible such as Heat*n*bond. Simply apply the fusible to the wrong side of your appliqué or accent fabric and trace your design—remember to mirror your design since you're drawing it on the back! Cut it out and then iron it onto your base fabric. By applying the fusible before cutting the shape, you'll prevent fraying and deforming of the appliqué fabric.

Premade appliqués are super convenient and might save you tears and time down the road!

COSPLAYER: Alchemical Cosplay

COSTUME: Astrologian
from *Final Fantasy XIV*

Photo by Solita D Photo

Heat transfer vinyl is widely available in tons of colors, shines, weights, and sizes. HTV permanently bonds to fabric with heat and provides a similar effect to fused fabric appliqués. This vinyl is very thin and has a super clean, crisp quality to it, making it a great choice for anime costumes and other sharp, more modern detailing. To apply, read the application instructions for your brand of vinyl and then use a pressing cloth and plenty of pressure on your iron or heat press.

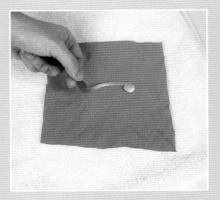

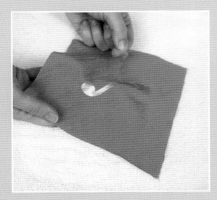

Beading

Incorporating beading into your dress embellishments can be as simple as adding random sparkle into an embroidered, lace, or colorwork design, or it can be as complex as a whole appliqué, all made from different kinds, shapes, and sizes of beads.

All you really need is a needle, thread, beads, and a lot of patience.

For inspiration, look at some of the more elaborate costumes from the *Game of Thrones* TV show, or historical garments worn by nobility. If you're going to do a large, elaborate piece like that, place it front and center and show it off on a bodice or tabard.

Smaller, more subtle lines or accents of beading can go anywhere on your gown, but like rhinestones, beads look best when they catch the light.

Proportion can also be tricky so draw out and plan where and how you want to place the beads. Nothing is worse than getting 10 hours into sewing bead accents and realizing that you need to do 10 more hours for a balanced look. Planning ahead also helps you choose the right size beads for the scale of the embellishment.

Beads don't always have to be beads— sequins and goldwork are great substitutes with their own super sparkly look. Sequins are easy to find, but goldwork—tiny tubes of shiny metal, which you can use as outlines or cut apart for textural "chips"—has to be bought from a specialist. Both can be applied with either a traditional needle and thread or a hook.

Tambour, Aari, and Lunéville are beading techniques that use a very similar tool and are often labeled interchangeably. They help you complete beading and embroidery much more quickly and efficiently than doing it by hand. The general technique is similar to latchhooking or wig ventilating, wherein a hook is used to do a chain stitch which beads, sequins, or goldwork can be loaded onto. It requires an investment in equipment (a hook and a larger embroidery frame or a tambour table), but if you plan on doing yards and yards of detailed beadwork, it can be worth the time and investment to learn!

Buttons and Closures

Closures don't always have to be functional; they can also be used as embellishments! Sometimes, it makes more sense to treat design elements like a laced bodice front, buttons on a sleeve cuff, ties at a waist or neckline, or other elements that look like closures as decorative items only and design the garment to open and close elsewhere.

This means that you don't have to treat the faux closure as a structural element and can instead construct it in a way that's pretty, balanced, and under no tension. The most common example of this is false fronts on bodices. Depending on your costume, it may make more sense to have a back zipper or button closure and then have the design closure be purely decorative, with pretty laces and no additional boning.

Another example is a large waist tie with a bow. Tying a bow that holds things closed and that is balanced, symmetrical, and shaped nicely can be difficult! Instead, use a standard closure for your garment and attach the ties or bows for decoration.

COSPLAYER: Cowbutt Crunchies
COSTUME: Button Knight
(original design)
Photo by Alexandra Lee Studios

Embroidery

Embroidery is a subject that can—and does—fill books of its own! Embroidery can be as simple as a single stitch or it can be entire yards of colors, stitches, and materials, covering entire skirts and panels. When approaching embroidering your ballgown, it's usually easier to consider the overall aesthetic when making choices: Is your character rich, poor, nobility, a warrior; is the gown more historical or more fantastic; are you looking for a handcrafted aesthetic or a shiny, perfect look? Let your understanding of your character guide you in specific decisions about color, patterns, and style.

Hand embroidery requires nothing but thread (usually embroidery floss) and a needle, but it can be used to create beautiful artisan results. It has a textured and personalized quality, and it allows you to incorporate beads or sequins into your stitching.

Machine embroidery can be done with home embroidery machines and most sewing machines. Home embroidery machines are super helpful for stitching large, multicolored, engineered pieces. If you have a newer sewing machine you will mostly likely have built-in decorative stitches, which are sewn in a straight line, perfect for stitching along hems and seams. You can also layer decorative stitches, mixing and matching threads, to create somewhat more complex patterns.

Machine embroidery is much faster than hand embroidery, but it tends to be flatter and denser; however, both are valuable ways to add your own touches to your cosplay.

Lace and Trims

Trims by the yard are some of the most common ways to embellish not just ballgowns but other kinds of formal wear. These usually come with repeating patterns and can be bought in the length you need, which makes them an easy way to dress up skirt hems, sleeve hems, or any other long edges. Finding the right trim for your design can be a little tricky, though, and it helps to know the different varieties of trim.

Lace comes in many forms, including lace fabric by the yard; lace trim by the foot or yard; lace appliqués; or even hybrid materials like lace-edged tulle or organza. For ballgown trim, narrow lace trim and appliqués are the most useful at the embellishment stage. We have a few favorite types of lace.

Venise Lace

This type of lace is characterized by its heavy, stand-alone lace patterns, with no backing. It's often designed with a flat edge, making it perfect for applying as trim, but can also come in other shapes. Common motifs are shells, swirls, leaves, and flowers. It can be hard to find Venise lace in colors besides white, black, creams, and metallics, but because it is usually one solid type of thread throughout and has no backing, it is easily dyed or painted to a specific color of your choice. This is a great, versatile lace for use all over your costume, including cuffs, necklines, in seams, and as borders for other, larger embellishments.

Alençon Lace

This lace has lighter, less solid designs on a net background, with edges of the pattern emphasized by a border of heavier thread or couching. It's commonly sold by the yard with two edges on one strip, which you can cut apart to create edging and border pieces. This lace usually comes in wider patterns than Venise lace and is sometimes additionally embellished with beads or sequins during manufacturing. This lace tends to come in more color varieties, which is good because it can be tricky to dye or paint because the backing also picks up that color. It's an excellent choice for decorating ballgown skirts because the proportions look nice even on the fluffiest of skirts.

Embroidered Lace

Embroidered lace is a catch-all term for a type of embellishment where lace patterns are embroidered onto a backing fabric, usually tulle or organza. Because it's not made like true lace, it can come in very wide designs, with the top of the swoops or designs reaching the full width of the yardage. Embroidered lace comes in a huge variety of colors and designs and the fanciest often have three-dimensional flowers, gemstones, and beading built in. While it's usually not designed for edging or trim the same way some other laces are, buying a few yards and carefully cutting it apart into smaller motifs can give you a lot of beautiful, fancy material to place however you like. This lace, however, is expensive.

Eyelet Lace and Other Cotton Laces

Almost more of a ribbon than a real lace, eyelet lace is usually a cotton or otherwise plain fabric embroidered with eyelets or holes that create a pattern. It's a more rustic, homey type of trim and is good for simpler dresses. It's also a great way to fancy up undergarments because it is soft and it breathes.

Lace Appliqué

This isn't a type of lace so much as it is a specific shape—appliqué can be bought or made in any of the common lace types. Instead of yardage, lace appliqué comes in a single motif shape and can be applied anywhere.

Rhinestones and Large Gems

Rhinestones and other gems are a great way to add sparkle and interest to your gown. While you can add gems anywhere on your costume, consider concentrating them in areas where they can give off the most visual impact—bodices, tabards, hair pieces, and accessories are all good options for a big effect without having to use thousands of stones.

Large Gems

Available online and at some craft stores, these gems, which are usually acrylic casts measuring between ½″ and 2″, can be found in three varieties: sew-on, flat back, and pointed back. Sew-on gems have small holes already in them and can be sewn anywhere on your garment, while flat back or pointed back gems must be mounted either with glue or in a bezel. When adding these gems to your dress, consider the fabric weight: a soft, drapey organza sleeve might not be the best place to add several gems, while the structured front of a bodice can take heavier embellishments with no problem. Gems can also be recolored with permanent pens or alcohol inks, so if you can't find the color you're looking for, consider buying colorless gems and coloring them yourself!

Rhinestones

Rhinestones are much smaller than regular acrylic gems, but tend to be much sparklier, especially in large numbers. They come in a variety of sizes as well, anywhere from 1mm to 10mm. The key to rhinestones' sparkle is their faceting—different parts of the surface catch light at different angles and give a twinkling effect at even subtle movement.

Glue-on rhinestones require glue added to each stone back individually and then are put onto the fabric or prop.

Hot-fix gemstones use a specialized tool with tips that heat up the rhinestone, activating adhesive on the back of the stone, which you can then press into place.

Both stones look identical—gluing the individual stones tends to be more secure but hot-fix stones are *much* faster to apply. You decide!

COSPLAYER: Cowbutt Crunchies
COSTUME: Loki from *Thor* (original design)
Photo by The World of Gwendana

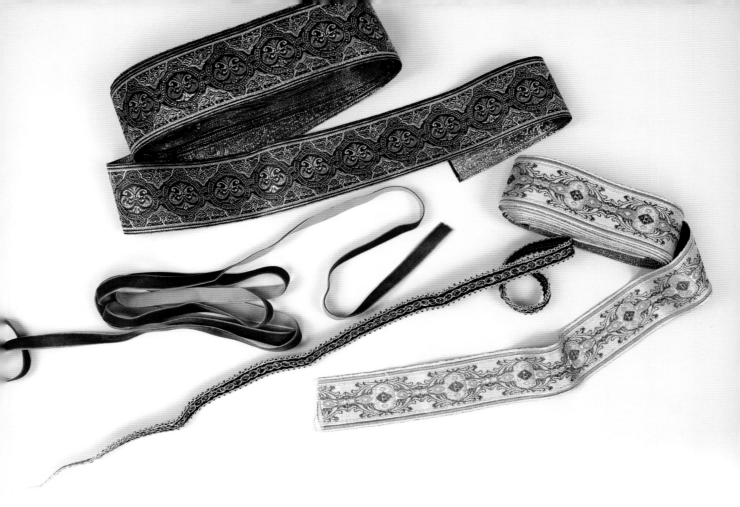

Ribbons

Ribbon isn't something we use as often as lace, but there are ways it can help your ballgowns and other formal wear shine. The two types of ribbons you may find most helpful are satin and jacquard ribbon.

Satin Ribbon

Satin ribbon is the shiny ribbon available at any craft or fabric store, available in widths as narrow as ⅛″ and up to several inches wide. Thin satin ribbon is a great option for ties that will show, since it's fancier than twill tape. It's also a great material to use if your bodice has a false corset closure, since the material looks lush and formal in a crisscross pattern. Wider satin ribbon can also be used to make bows, especially for headpieces, sleeves, or other smaller areas where hemming fabric to make a bow might create very bulky shapes.

Jacquard Ribbon

Jacquard ribbon is a straight-edged ribbon with bright, colorful embroidery that covers the whole ribbon. It comes in a huge variety of colors, patterns, and widths. It's a great choice for medieval or fantasy costumes as it feels less modern than some other trims. Because it tends to be stiff, it's best to use it along straight edges.

WHEN TO ATTACH YOUR EMBELLISHMENTS

Embellishments can look lovely, but unsightly topstitching is a faux pas! Don't wait until the last minute to attach your embellishments; lace, beading and other trims should be sewn on before the lining layer is attached. Waiting until the ballgown is fully assembled will force you to sew through all layers of the gown, which will result in visible stitching on the underside of the lining and may cause puckering or pulling due to tension issues. Instead, add your embellishments early by hand or machine, stitching them through only the fashion and interlining fabrics. While the stitching on these fabrics may be unsightly, it will be covered by the lining layer for an expert finish.

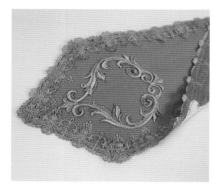  

Tip

Attach hem trim when you add the lining for a flawless finish with no visible stitching.

 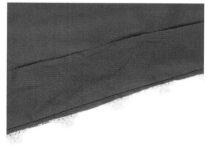 

1. Align the bottom edge of the fashion fabric and the trim, with right sides together.

2. Align the bottom edge of the fashion fabric and the lining, with right sides together, so that the trim is between them. Pin and stitch together ¼″ from the edge.

3. Turn the pieces right side out. Press the seams.

Cosplay Creative: Lunar Rose Costuming

Instagram: @lunarrosecostuming

As someone who primarily makes historically inspired costumes, I like the old adage that you should learn the rules enough to break them. While I personally enjoy the process of researching historical fashion and teaching myself period sewing techniques, I also like to use as many modern conveniences and resources as I can during my construction process. Time, budget, venue, and whether the costume will be entered into a cosplay competition are all factors I consider when deciding how historically accurate a project needs to be. For example, synthetic materials are often much easier to clean than more historically accurate silks. And while I frequently use modern metal eyelets and plastic boning for historical corsets, it is important that my foundation garments be correct for the time period of the costume.

COSPLAYER: Lunar Rose Costuming

COSTUME: Sugar Plum Fairy from *The Nutcracker*

Photo by Pixie Vision Photography

To be clear, there is a time and a place for historically accurate clothing. Museum interpreters and historical educators frequently use clothing as a means of storytelling to help modern people understand aspects of life in the past. In these situations, there is value in stitching a garment by hand or in selecting a material similar to what might have been historically available, because the clothing is part of your teaching toolbox. But if you are creating a historically inspired project for a convention or other type of non-educational event, how much time and effort you put into achieving historical accuracy is entirely up to you. Just enjoy the learning process and do the best you can!

Footwear

Pumps, booties, slippers, Mary Janes. and even historical shoes are all appropriate shoes for ballgowns. A complementary shoe is especially important if your feet are visible underneath a shorter or open hoop gown—in these cases, avoid clashing styles or incorrectly colored footwear. Some cosplayers enjoy decorating their own custom shoes in order to perfectly match their cosplays. Paint and embellishments can create a fun, secret detail that is only revealed when a cosplayer lifts those long skirts.

However, comfort is king, and we never recommend sacrificing comfort for style! When selecting a shoe, always choose one that fits well and that you would be comfortable wearing around a busy con for many hours. A beautiful gown is no fun to wear when your feet are aching. Remember that most people never see your feet under an enormous gown unless you choose to show them off. In this case, comfortable sneakers, platforms, and other padded, nontraditional shoes are great options that will secretly keep your feet feeling great all day!

Tip

Always select your footwear before hemming your gown and making any alterations! Be sure to wear your chosen shoes during the fitting, trimming, and finishing process.

TO HEEL OR NOT TO HEEL?

Even if your feet aren't visible, don't just immediately reach for flats! Heels or platforms add several inches to your height, which in turn creates an optical illusion of longer legs and a higher waist. This is an easy trick to create a more extreme silhouette, especially for cosplayers who might be on the shorter side. Wedges, flat platforms, or even hidden heel sneakers are fantastic ways to ride high in style without sacrificing cosplay comfort.

Walking

Ballgowns that sweep the floor can be a challenge to walk in without accidentally stepping on those long skirts. Take extra care to avoid tripping over your skirt or accidentally tearing a hole in the delicate fabric.

GOOD POSTURE

Maintaining good posture can go a long way toward keeping your skirts intact. Slouching or slumping forward will cause your skirts to droop and hit the ground, which can be dangerous. Instead, keep your back straight or even lean backward slightly when walking.

LIFT YOUR SKIRTS

For extra-long gowns or simply for faster walking, lifting your skirts is an easy trick to prevent tripping. However, simply lifting the outer skirt layer won't do much good if your petticoats are still riding close to the floor. Instead, bend over and gently grasp all layers of your skirt, including the undergarments. Avoid crumpling the skirt in your fists as this can create wrinkles. Straighten your back and bring the skirts up with you. The area in front of your feet should now be completely clear.

Sitting

Sitting in a large ballgown can be a challenge, even for experienced cosplayers! In general, avoid tight, crowded areas and look for seats where your gown will not impose on others. The ends of rows or isolated chairs provide more maneuverability.

PETTICOATS

To sit in a petticoat, approach the chair to sit as per normal. Lean forward and pull your skirt slightly higher and smooth out the back of your skirt to try to eliminate any buckling or folding. Hold the skirt in place and then sit. This method should help prevent uncomfortable pulling and will also help eliminate accidentally wrinkling the back of the gown.

HOOP SKIRTS

Sitting in a hoop skirt is slightly trickier and always requires additional space. Make sure that you have at least two or three chairs' worth of room before attempting to sit.

Lean down and gently grasp the back of your skirt with one hand, making sure that you have picked up all layers, including the hoop skirt. Straighten your back and lift upward. Turn and sit toward the front edge of the chair and drop the skirts behind you. The back of your hoop skirt should now be resting on the chair, with the rest of the skirt sloped out in front of you.

Photography and Posing

Your ballgown is constructed beautifully and it's finally time to show the world what you've created! Many cosplayers choose to wear their creations to anime and sci fi conventions, which sometimes involves posing for impromptu photographs for interested fans or partaking in more formal cosplay photo shoots with hired photographers. Both types of photo shoots are a great way to document and share your work with other cosplayers, while also creating a fantastic keepsake.

Before wearing your ballgown to a photo shoot or convention, try practicing a handful of poses at home in a mirror. This will help you find a comfortable pose and will also help commit that position to muscle memory. Enormous gowns can limit your range of motion so finding a favorite pose might be tricky. To help, try the following tips.

* When choosing a pose, consider your character's personality. Is your character peppy? Demure? Are they from a particular era in history? Allow this information to inform your body and let that personality shine through!

* Avoid static or stiff positioning. Front-facing positioning with little bend or movement can often turn out stiff or unnatural. Instead, add some life to your pose by introducing asymmetry. Avoid locking your joints and instead bend your elbows and wrists slightly for a natural-looking shape. For a more advanced pose, try arching your back as well to introduce even more movement.

COSPLAYER: Ilabelle Cosplay
COSTUME: Belle from *Beauty and the Beast*
Photo by Mama Kat Photography

For a fantastic beginner's pose, try a three-quarter view. Turn your body away from the camera, halfway between a front-facing pose and a profile pose, so only about three-fourths of your body is visible. Then tilt your head slightly back toward the camera. This is a highly flattering position that looks great on most cosplayers!

Extended arms are a great complement to extra-large ballgowns. Grand, elegant arm poses help reflect the sheer size of your cosplay and can create an overall balanced photograph. Lifting your arms in opposite directions is another trick to create a larger-than-life illusion while keeping a pose that feels natural and airy.

Don't forget about your legs! Even though they may be hidden, posing your legs and feet will help infuse a natural shape throughout your entire body. For a simple start, separate your legs slightly and shift your weight onto one foot.

For formal or shy characters, try a painterly or sweet position. Clasped hands or a gentle touch to your shoulder or face are interesting options that can help bring a photograph to life.

Does your pose feel stiff? Shake it out! If your body starts to feel rigid, don't force it. Instead, relax, take a moment to breathe, and try again.

And finally, have fun! Your love of cosplay and your amazing gown will show through in those photographs!